KANDINSKY

KANDINSKY

by

Ramon Tio Bellido

Translated by Jane Brenton

PORTLAND HOUSE
NEW YORK

Originally published by Fernand Hazan, Paris 1986

This edition published 1988 by Portland House
Distributed by Crown Publishers, Inc.
225 Park Avenue South
New York, New York 10003

Copyright © Fernand Hazan, Paris 1986
Copyright © ADAGP
English Translation Copyright © Bestseller Publications Ltd, 1988

All rights reserved. No part of this publication
may be reproduced, stored in a retrieval system,
or transmitted, in any form or by any means, electronic,
mechanical, photocopying, recording or otherwise,
without the prior permission of the copyright holder.

ISBN 0-517-64793-1

Printed and bound in Hong Kong

h g f e d c b

Vassily Kandinsky is generally regarded as the founder of abstract painting; perhaps it would be more appropriate to describe him as its discoverer – in the sense that an archaeologist may be the discoverer of a cave full of prehistoric paintings.

According to Kandinsky himself, he painted his first 'abstract watercolour' in 1910. That date has been disputed, but, to us today, the debate appears of purely academic interest. It no longer matters crucially whether he was the first person to paint a picture entirely unconcerned with the representation of reality; what is important is to understand his absolute dedication, throughout his life, to ridding himself of the 'object', the whole world of external appearances.

At the time when Kandinsky, 'that late-comer to painting', embarked on his quest, European intellectuals and writers, in the fields of literature and music as well as the plastic arts, were already capitalizing on the innovations of their predecessors, and moving away from 'subject matter' as their reference point. Analysing the 'object' became the pretext for painting, while writing and melody were broken down into their elements and assumed new forms.

What the avant-garde demanded was a great freedom *vis-à-vis* reality.

Impressionism was the first art historical movement to manifest this tendency, both in its rejection of anecdotal and narrative content, and in making the impression created by a chosen subject – not the subject itself – the *raison d'être* of painting.

In taking the actual processes of representation as the subject matter of painting, the Impressionists paved the way for Cubism, Constructivism and all those movements concerned to explore the image as a function of its various characteristics.

Equally, the resulting emphasis on individual freedom of interpretation – claimed in fact by artists since the time of the Romantics – meant that there were virtually no constraints on what could be painted, beyond the limitations of creativity itself. Symbolism, and to a degree Expressionism, aimed to demonstrate the superior reality of art, as a domain within which the imagination was paramount.

The quintessence of imaginative truth is abstraction – the artist's capacity to extract from concrete reality, or the natural world, something that is not a copy but a concept, or Platonic ideal. In turning away from the realistic model, eliminating any reference to recognizable reality, 'abstract' art seeks to discover an essence. Its sole concern is to create a pictorial (or literary or musical) object that exists, finally, for its own sake, which obeys its own rules – which 'discovers the internal necessity of the harmony it establishes within itself'.

The more the artist detaches himself from an external 'objective' model, the more he must rely on the purely subjective model suggested by his own nature, or spirituality (what Kandinsky calls 'inner necessity').

This absence of a 'concrete' object gives rise to a dislocation of perception, a confusion; since the artist alone determines the emotional and aesthetic criteria by which he operates, his actions appear at first sight to be entirely arbitrary.

In this context, it is revealing to recall Kandinsky's own confusion on first seeing Monet's *Haystack at Giverny*, which was exhibited in Moscow in 1895. Kandinsky declared: '. . . it was from the catalogue I learned this was a haystack. I was upset I had not recognized it. I also thought the painter had no right to paint in such an imprecise fashion. Dimly I was aware too that the object did not appear in the picture . . .'

The experience may have come as a shock to Kandinsky, but it also spurred him to action, urging him – paradoxically – in the direction of still greater abstraction. It is as

Kandinsky *c.*1900

though he wanted to exorcise the feelings of unease he experienced when confronting the object concealed in Monet's mists of colour, and which he found himself totally unable to decipher.

The point of the anecdote lies in the paradox. Kandinsky, who at that point in his life had not yet decided to make painting his career, was shocked by the absence of structure and construction in a pictorial object that existed only in terms of the orchestration of its colours. His ignorance of the codes of the Impressionist aesthetic prevented him, literally, from seeing the object, which bore little resemblance to its counterpart in the real world. And if his failure in this respect confirmed him in his desire to seek the elimination of concrete references altogether – however implicitly stated – it also pointed graphically to the limitations of abstraction, namely its limited intelligibility. Others, indeed, regarded the option of banishing figuration altogether as an over-reaction, a fundamental error. Various intermediate solutions were devised, among them those adopted by Cubism, and the altogether more intuitive approach of Matisse – who, without denying the object completely, nevertheless decomposed it to the point of rendering it practically unintelligible; in his radical revisions of the pictorial system, he too demonstrated an absolute freedom of expression.

By comparison with these other more analytical and pragmatic approaches, Kandinsky's unique contribution was to raise art to a metaphysical dimension.

In the search for a mystical 'type', independent of contingent reality, the crucial elements at the artist's disposal were colour and form, which he must employ 'to best effect', so that they were in perfect harmony with his inner experience. Art, in order to attain universal significance, needed to become more ascetic, exclude ornament and rhetoric, and so arrive at a combination of elements having no meaning outside their context within the whole – that whole itself having significance only as a function of the spiritual quest of its creator. In such an approach, there is, of course, an inherent difficulty: that the artist, in attempting to free himself from the restraints of reality, will cut himself off from it entirely. It was the problem that soon confronted Kandinsky; he explains that he began by making the concrete abstract, in a process of 'rarification', but was then forced to concretize the abstract, through 'reification'.

Kandinsky aimed to make the work of art the expression of the innermost being of its creator. Klee was perhaps more clear-thinking when he pointed out that such expression was still a part of nature – even if it could not readily be recognized as such; that it was germane to the creative process, which consisted in proceeding from model to matrix, tracing the origins of things in *natura naturans* – nature in process, not nature in its evolved form. But on that point Kandinsky was in fundamental disagreement with his friend. He did not accept that the goal of art was to work backwards from the much-despised model, to reveal its primitive forms and ultimate genesis. Rather, his artistic philosophy was rooted in the conviction that the constituent elements of art were universal, that they existed independently and in perpetuity; only in being brought into a synthesis with the creative gesture could they enter the world of tangible realities.

One can see the logic of this position – especially if one accepts, with Kandinsky, that art is an autonomous language, governed by its own set of rules. Also, one is inclined to be the more sympathetic to it because of the struggle the supporters of abstraction faced in presenting their views, greeted as they were with incomprehension and hostility on all sides. Undoubtedly their case was not helped by a central confusion – a failure to make any distinction between Art itself and the specific work of art.

For, whatever theoretical justification may be adopted for this or that type of expression, the function of each individual work of art must be to communicate – to give 'material form' even to that which is 'non-material'.

It may be appropriate at this point to say something about the psychology of Kandinsky himself, for he was very much a product of his Slav and Russian cultural background, greatly influenced by Symbolism of a highly Romantic variety, and sympathetic to the traditions of theosophy. For Kandinsky, the Spiritual was a progressive force. Appearances were more than deceptive, they were positively misleading, serving to conceal the truth of Reality. The World was an arena for the interplay of forces of psychic energy, impossible to describe or even perceive except through riddles of simile and synthesis. The only way to penetrate to the 'sense of the spirit of things . . .', to achieve 'pure Art', was by means of analogy. Where Picasso, Braque, and even Klee, attempted to express truth in art through metonymy (working from the specific to the general), Kandinsky's mental and artistic universe was founded in metaphor, as a means of reflecting the primary image of an omnipotent, unknowable Spirituality.

How then could Kandinsky hope to make these obscure creative processes understood? The solution lay in the written word. With all its defects, it provided the one sure way of communicating his intentions as he embarked on the highly controversial course of eliminating all traditional figurative references from his work.

Like many another artist at the turn of the century, Kandinsky was a prolific writer. Of course, the publication of theoretical texts and aesthetic manifestos was nothing new, and indeed these things have been commonplace since the time of the Renaissance. The history of modern art is punctuated by articles, open letters to supporters or detractors, polemics, pamphlets and manifestos. But much of this literary production was at one remove, often the work of people whose job it was to write. Poets, philosophers, academicians, scholars and critics routinely issued their analyses and pronouncements on the contemporary artistic scene, but always from the perspective of someone not himself involved directly in the pictorial process.

For the artist, understandably, the effect was to make him wish to resume control of his own destiny, so that he felt an increasing obligation to take responsibility not only for his creative activities but also for the reception of his work by the public. He was forced into the position of becoming a writer himself.

To put it another way, it became difficult, if not actually impossible, for the artist to explain himself through a third party. If he were not to be misunderstood – or wilfully misrepresented – he had to take the risk of entering the lists as a theoretician on his own behalf. For Kandinsky, the forming of images had to work hand in hand with the formulation of ideas.

Necessary allies, the two processes complement each other in the pursuit of greater clarity. Yet they are very far from being interchangeable. The words do not provide a key to the images, nor do they set out a programme which the images proceed to illustrate.

When he attempted to give an account of his artistic philosophy in *Concerning the Spiritual in Art*, of 1910, Kandinsky turned to music – by its nature a non-figurative art form – as the peg on which to hang his ideas.

In the course of the nineteenth century, as the power of the naturalistic image in painting began to wane, so music had tended to give the lead to the other arts. No doubt this was in part because of the appeal of its rigorous underlying structure, but also because of its ability to address the senses, to speak directly to the soul.

Many artists and writers were misled by these affinities and began to juggle with systems of correspondences, trying to establish exact parallels between the principles

Concerning the Spiritual in Art, cover for the first edition

of musical composition and those of plastic expression. Goethe, who was among the first to attempt this task, concluded that such mechanistic comparisons were doomed to failure; he nevertheless regretted that painting did not have, like music, its 'ground-bass' – by which he meant that it did not have a reliable theoretical basis that would permit an objective evaluation of its principles of composition.

Kandinsky called his first non-figurative pictures *Composition* and *Improvisation*, both musical terms. Obviously these were not arrived at by chance, and they have caused endless confusion and misunderstanding. One must pose the question: were Kandinsky's frequent incursions into musical terminology merely allusions to the power of music to move the spirit, part of an attempt, by analogy, to inject a spiritual dimension into painting, or did they reflect a conscious decision on his part to establish a basic theory of pictorial composition, remedying the deficiency regretted years before by Goethe? Unfortunately, there is no simple answer. Convenient though it would be to come down on one side or the other, a detailed study of Kandinsky's writings and paintings does not support either view to the exclusion of the other. Any explanation is bound to take account of the often conflicting evidence offered by these two very different modes of expression.

The central responsibility for the confusion lies with Kandinsky himself. To take only one obvious example, *Concerning the Spiritual* opens with a review of the contemporary arts that is intended as a sort of introductory exposition of the fundamental drive towards 'dematerialization'. It is full of abstract references to the nature of sounds and tonalities, both in the way they are perceived and the vibrations they set up, and in their ability to engender a loss of meaning. Through an analysis of the force of 'word-sounds' in the work of Maeterlinck, and the use of the *leitmotiv* in the music of Wagner, Kandinsky deduces that repetition gives a word a different meaning and weight from the usual, so that it then enters a 'more supernatural' sphere, and benefits from a 'spiritual atmosphere'. Extending his argument, he goes on to discuss Mussorgsky, Debussy and Schoenberg, establishing a distinction between a 'beautiful exterior' and a 'beautiful interior', towards which latter, he says, 'we are impelled by an inner necessity, once only we have renounced conventional forms of Beauty'. That necessity is expressed in music as dissonance and, ultimately, atonality, both of which seem shocking and ugly to anyone who is attracted only by surface appearances and imitation, and who does not admit as '. . . sacred all those processes by which [the artist's personality] is revealed . . .'.

Kandinsky, sketch, 1923

Turning finally to painting, he condemns utterly the Neo-Impressionist movement, which he accuses of erecting into a dogmatic system the naturalistic tendencies of its predecessors. Only Rossetti, Böcklin, Cézanne, Matisse and Picasso escape his strictures, for a variety of different but related reasons: 'all these artists search for the internal content within external forms.' Cézanne through his '. . . abstract, often mathematical formulas, from which emerges a shining harmony . . .', Matisse who, with his gifts as a colourist, paints pictures of '. . . subtle beauty . . . full of delight, purely melodic . . .', Picasso by his boldness and his attempt to achieve structure '. . . with the aid of numerical relationships . . .', these being the foundations of Cubism (although Kandinsky finds it astonishing that the movement still chose to preserve the '. . . material appearance').

'Vibration', 'harmony', 'tonality', 'sonority' – all these terms are used to describe colour and form, making explicit the parallel with the 'grammar' of music. Given the consistency with which the words are used, Kandinsky's intentions seem, on the face of it, quite clear. It is thus tempting simply to assume, as others have done, that his purpose was indeed to construct a universal theory of art, borrowing from musical terminology in order to construct a metaphor that would provide the justification for his own artistic practices.

Unfortunately, Kandinsky elsewhere dismisses the validity of that approach. Certainly he was strongly predisposed to devise a set of fixed rules for painting, by seeking to establish a series of precise parallels with the laws of musical composition, but at the end of his treatise he casts doubt on the feasibility of the enterprise. '. . . Harmony as it is practised today would appear to make it more difficult than ever, at the present time, to elaborate a perfect, comprehensive theory, to create an established "thorough-bass" of painting.' In much the same vein he was to write a few years later (in his autobiography *Reminiscences*): '. . . if the problem of form existed in principle, then a solution to it could be found. And all those who knew the solution would be in a position to create works of art, which would mean that art would no longer exist . . .'

In other words, he effectively concedes that no one inflexible theory of art is possible, that there can be no lexicon or grammar that will provide the key to creating a work of art, and that it is therefore destined to remain essentially mysterious and indefinable, inaccessible to any theory, however perfectly devised.

Thus Kandinsky appears to contradict the drift of much that he wrote elsewhere. But the truth is probably far more simple: he does not in fact renounce his desire to find a justification of his beliefs, any more than he renounces the beliefs themselves. 'Music has a grammar,' he wrote, 'a grammar which, like any living thing, changes over long periods of time, and yet can always usefully be referred to, much in the way you consult a dictionary . . .' Descartes, it may be remembered, said something rather similar about Nature a few decades earlier.

But Kandinsky, together with a few other bold spirits, faced an entirely different situation: they were attempting now to free themselves from nature, as a means of escaping from figuration. Kandinsky was first and foremost a painter, and one cannot look at what he wrote without bearing that in mind. The theoretician cannot be regarded in isolation from the artist. In the last analysis, the writing is only a secondary response to the primary matter of painting. Kandinsky's texts must be read, therefore, as attempted rationalizations, both as tentative and as contradictory as the progress of the work itself, valuable only in so far as they are a record of his determination to spell out a truth about painting. It would be pointless, and indeed misconceived, to seek to discover in his writings any perfect all-embracing theory, any stringent conceptual analysis that is going to 'explain' the moment in the history of art when the extraordinary and difficult transition to abstraction was taking place. The texts may be full of gaps, often vague, reliant on intuition, sometimes irritating because of their metaphysical flavour and omission of any social or historical context, but, if anything, that is added confirmation that they exist as an extension of the painting, and in reflecting it, also cast light upon it.

It is apparent from a study of Kandinsky's *oeuvre* that his painting evolved from the stylization of the figure through to its atomization and eventual disintegration. This did not occur entirely as a product of the decision to reject imitative art; it also proceeded via the multiplication, diversification and repetition of the drawn forms on the canvas. In time, Kandinsky ceased to look at his frame of representation as a defined area of 'space', and began to see it instead as a field of tensions, in which various forces played and interacted. His vision of painting became dynamic rather than static.

The representation of motion in his work was a function of the introduction of a temporal dimension.

By that we do not mean to imply a literal animation of the image (that would be closer to the concerns of kinetic art), nor to suggest that these elements may be found in the actual processes of the fabrication of the work (as would be the case for example in the gestural painting of the Abstract Expressionists). Rather does the temporal dimension make itself felt through a lack of fixed reference points within the image, forcing the observer to enter into the composition in order to understand it, to penetrate the image in an 'erratic progress'. Undoubtedly it is that revolution in perception that has been the principal contribution of abstract art. The feeling aroused by abstract paintings – and particularly Kandinsky's – is not so much the disturbing sense that they are at once familiar and yet infinitely strange, it is the experience of a fundamental loss of self, a profound disorientation. The subject of the painting is *not* the object, indeed there may be no object present; rather it is something we have to reconstruct for ourselves. In a curious way, the image we contemplate confers on us its own powers of invention.

BEFORE PAINTING

'Stick to the facts!' is a perfectly sound maxim if you happen to be a historian of the positivist school. It is not so easy to put into practice if you are writing a critical study of an artist. About Kandinsky, we know relatively little, partly because he did not commit himself to a career as a painter until he reached the age of thirty. He was, anyway, of a retiring disposition and disliked publicity and social events. When he referred to his private life, which was rarely, it was always in the briefest possible terms. Kandinsky was not a public man, and even his appearance – a sartorial elegance that amounted almost to dandyishness – was enough to put many people off. They tended to find him cold, distant, something of a snob.

In his private life there was little that was remarkable. No major crises or scandals for the biographer to delve into. None of those racy details that make a good story and reinforce the popular stereotype of the artist as a bohemian and a rebel. To those who like to have their prejudices confirmed, or who enjoy larger-than-life characters, Kandinsky will come as a sad disappointment: his image simply does not fit.

Given, then, that so little is known about the events of Kandinsky's life, one is bound to make some attempt to explore the influences that helped to shape his personality. Since hard facts are in short supply, how else can one begin to understand what it was that made him recognize himself as an artist, and then take the radical step of changing his life in order to become one? A purely psychological analysis is unlikely to meet with much success on its own (unless under the strict conditions of psychoanalysis, in which the unconscious is laid bare), and nor can one rely wholly on an explanation rooted in cultural determinism (an exploration of the artist's heritage, and its refinement through education and experience).

In order to do justice to the extraordinary adventure that was abstraction, in which Kandinsky was a pioneer, we must clearly not neglect any possible avenue of approach. It would be folly not to take advantage of such documentation as is available about Kandinsky's life and history, and indeed the broader historical background as well. For undoubtedly all these things, events in the public or private life, whether traumatic or merely routine, must have their effect on the individual and influence his personality, and with it the course of his work.

Obviously there is a limit to our ability to understand Kandinsky as a personality – as an individual – yet time and time again we come up against the evidence of his single-mindedness, his obsessive pursuit of spiritual enlightenment, reflected both in the quiet persistence of his aesthetic engagement, and in a life-style biased towards introspection and meditation.

Such traits of character may sound unattractive. Kandinsky has indeed been much reproached for his idealism and egocentricity, which prevented him from seeing reality except through the distorting prism of his own convictions and beliefs. It is impossible to deny that his mysticism caused him to be less than discerning about the affairs and conflicts of the real world.

Without wishing to leap ahead, it may be appropriate here to look at one particular illustration of the intimate inter-relation that existed between his life and work – and which on occasion had profound consequences. In 1915,

Kandinsky was in Russia. It may have been in part because of problems in his personal life, or because he found it an emotional strain to readjust to the realities of Holy Mother Moscow, but in that whole year Kandinsky produced not one single picture. Nothing, in fact, beyond a few water-colours and sketches – 'in order not to lose my touch.' Some biographers explain this inactivity by the difficulty of finding suitable materials in the declining years of the Czarist regime, when Russia was not only engaged in a world war but was also in the grip of pre-Revolutionary fervour and disorder. For the want of a nail the shoe was lost, runs the old proverb, and superficially it seems an attractive enough explanation. But it is unlikely to be the whole truth. Reality is rarely that simple. If Russia was in an unstable condition, so too was Kandinsky. The war had taken him by surprise. His humanist beliefs were all directed towards the establishment on earth of a 'New Spirit', yet he found himself confronted by the greatest barbarity of them all. The war was not to be, as his friend Franz Marc – and, by implication, Kandinsky himself – hoped, a 'salutary interlude [which would] cleanse Europe and keep her alert'. He was profoundly disillusioned, his impassioned idealism shaken to its foundations. 'I thought that the terrain of the future would be swept clean in quite another way. The price of the cleansing is atrocious,' he replied to his friend. Poverty and shortages alone are not the explanation for the interruption in his artistic activity. The death and destruction of the battlefields confronted him with a cruel reality such as he had never envisaged, judging by the optimistic vision of humanity that underlies his theories of abstraction.

With hindsight, such blindness appears a staggering act of self-deception. But Kandinsky himself was not wholly to blame. He was not the only one to be so mistaken, and what is more, he was truly shaken and repentant when he discovered the truth. His error was due more to naïveté than active complicity. One might remember the Italian Futurists, who in a very direct sense eased the path of Mussolini's Fascism. To put the matter in its perspective, Kandinsky believed in 'progress', as a means of recalling everyone to a sense of his responsibilities, but it was a progress confined to the spiritual sphere. Such a belief may seem alien to us, conditioned as we are to a very different set of instincts and rationalizations. In the West, a religious man nevertheless engages with the issues of public debate, and suits his behaviour and ideas to the requirements of the times; the contemplative goes armed, if only with his rhetoric. The Slav temperament could hardly be more different – and, without descending into cliché, Kandinsky was a typical Slav; he believed above all in transcendance and the supernatural essence of things.

Here we touch on a point that is crucial to any understanding of Kandinsky's philosophy and its expression in art. The accents of modernity in his painting are familiar and unmistakeable, but we are also required to respond on another level, to something that is outside of time, something that cannot be stated directly. It is this 'inscrutable' expression of an eternal and essential truth, inaccessible to discursive thought, that makes his work so very difficult to comprehend, especially given the initial paradox that there is no 'object' in the picture to serve as a basis for understanding.

Vassily Kandinsky was born in Moscow in 1866, the son of a cultivated middle class family. His parents moved soon after his birth to Odessa, and separated in 1871. Kandinsky was brought up by his aunt, Elisabeth Tikheev. His childhood was calm and studious. Every winter he visited his father in Moscow, and back at home in Odessa he learned the piano and the 'cello, essential accomplishments for anyone of his background. At the age of thirteen he was given his first box of paints, a set of tubes of watercolour.

Kandinsky as a student in Munich, *c.*1900

His family seem to have accepted his artistic leanings, although we do not know if he received positive encouragement. Certainly he grew up in an atmosphere where such talents were not regarded as unusual: '. . . [his] mother played the piano, his father the zither, [he] had sketched since he was a child, regularly visited exhibitions, and was a collector in a small way . . .'

Kandinsky, however, chose to enrol as a student of law and economics. He made a special study of Russian and Roman law, drawing some novel conclusions from a comparison of the two systems.

In 1889, the Society of Natural Sciences, Ethnography and Anthropology sent him on a field-trip to Vologda, the capital of the most northerly province in Russia, north of Moscow. He returned with a memorandum on 'Pagan recollections in the religion of the Finnish Surie tribes'. But once again he derived unexpected benefits from a prescribed task; his treatise was not to be the only thing of consequence he brought back from the expedition.

That same year he travelled for the first time to Paris, where he visited the World Fair. Three years later – when he was twenty-six – he married his cousin Ania Shemiakina, in a Russian Orthodox ceremony. In 1893, he taught in the Faculty of Law of the University of Moscow, and the following year took over the direction of a printing firm. In 1896, he turned down a university post in Estonia and went to live in Munich, intent on becoming a full time painter.

Those, starkly, are the facts. But they raise more questions than they answer. Behind the bland recital of the events of a life is concealed another unspoken reality that is far less accessible, and also far more interesting. If we knew about that, we would be able to satisfy our curiosity as to what it was that motivated Kandinsky from the first, and maintained him on the course that led inexorably to his eventual decision to be an artist.

It is like a riddle which we have to try to unravel. Perhaps the explanation lies in some form of dual personality, whose tortuous logic escapes us . . .? Certainly there is an inevitability about the whole thing that suggests it was not a rational matter. But then what was it that made Kandinsky delay his decision for so long? To put it down to his conformist upbringing, or to conclude that he was immature and a procrastinator by nature (effectively the same argument, since both are a reflection of his affluent circumstances), does not begin to explain the change that suddenly came over him, leading him to alter the whole course of his life and work.

In fact any such notion is invalidated by subsequent events. Kandinsky was no activist, no social revolutionary, even of the armchair variety, but he demonstrated a considerable degree of passion and commitment in defending his artistic beliefs, and he played a full part in the often thankless campaigns of the avant-garde.

Psychoanalytic theory would have it that we are all subject to a process of 'sublimation', that each individual represses certain of his desires and directs them into an externalizing activity such as art. One wonders, what were the pressures to which Kandinsky was subject, that it took him thirty years to achieve that liberation and branch out as an artist? Once again his own statements are of little help. The thirty years in Russia are practically a blank sheet in Kandinsky's memory, and few real clues emerge. His recollection of events is in fact highly selective. Perhaps it is not surprising that the anecdotes he chooses to remember all in some sense anticipate his eventual artistic career. No one seems to have thought to question him about this almost schizoid split between his life and beliefs during that curiously featureless period of his early existence. As it is, all that is remarkable is his patient resolve in awaiting the hour of his destiny . . .

We know that Kandinsky's father used to go regularly

Kandinsky, draft
for the catalogue cover
of *Der Blaue Reiter*,
1912

to exhibitions. Did his son never accompany him? Did he never see the work of Répine and Surikov, those pale reflections of the popular Realism of Courbet? Did he not see the illuminated compositions of Vrubel, form an opinion about the baroque luxuriance of his palette and the exaggerated symbolism of his themes? There is not a word about any of this. Apparently all he could think about was the nostalgic magic of the paint box he was given as an adolescent, and the sense of wonder he experienced from the indefinable sensation when '... the brush with its inflexible will ... gave birth with each gash of colour to a musical tonality.' We know also that he was fascinated by the inner incandescence and luminosity of the paintings of Rembrandt, which he saw at the Hermitage Museum in St Petersburg, and once again overwhelmed with emotion at the sight of the frescoes in the *isbas* of Vologda, whose polychromatic effects gave him '... the impression of penetrating into colour, advancing into the interior of a picture'.

Everything we learn suggests a vivid reponsiveness to matters of the spirit, a visionary temperament, and a love of colour – which Kandinsky regarded as the best means of expressing mystical experience, a way of attaining a superior reality in art, beyond the feeble deception of appearances. His acute sensibility was apparent even in his studies, in, for example, his preference for popular Russian law, which offered 'a liberation and a solution based on fundamental Justice', and which, he said, led him to 'exercise that necessary capacity for profound study in the subtly material sphere which is called the sphere of the abstract'. One can only begin to speculate how harsh and corrupt the official judicial system of the Czars must have been in comparison ...

Obsessed with the memory of an unrecognizable haystack, and possessed of resources amply sufficient to meet his needs, Kandinsky left for Munich – his choice of destination explained by his admiration for Germany and the high reputation of art schools in the Bavarian capital.

MUNICH–MURNAU–MUNICH
TRAVELS AND THE BLAUE REITER

Once arrived in Munich, Kandinsky enrolled at the private art school run by the painter Anton Azbè, where he studied life-drawing, sketching and anatomy, regarded then as the fundamentals of an artistic education. He rapidly found the narrowness of the curriculum frustrating, and moved to another school as a pupil of Franz von Stuck, a leading figure in the Symbolist movement. Although he appreciated the personal qualities of his tutor and respected his abilities, it was not long before he decided to opt out altogether and follow his own course, painting directly from the motif. 'In the period when I found studio work disappointing and I painted out of doors, I did mainly landscapes ... In my studies I let myself go. I didn't think much about houses, or trees, I applied streaks and blobs of colours onto the canvas with a palette knife and I made them sing with all the intensity I could ...' Once again, it is the expressive power of colour that Kandinsky singles out; it was to be the dominant characteristic of his work in the ensuing period. Indeed, he demonstrated such ability as a colourist that some have chosen to regard him at this point in his life as espousing Fauve or Expressionist theories. In fact that was not at all where Kandinsky's interest lay; rather his concentration on colour indicates to what extent, without even being conscious of it, he was already losing interest in reality and the natural world, which made so little impression on him that his whole concentration was focused on the surprising forms assumed by the thick pigments, modelled under the broad strokes of his palette knife. It was a new perception, detached from the external world, and it demanded a wholly different order of com-

Kandinsky and his pupils at the Phalanx School
(at the Gabriele Münter centre) in 1902–1903

position. Although at heart a believer in rules and discipline, from the first Kandinsky felt the need to keep his distance from academism; it was a decision arrived at instinctively, reflecting an inner conviction that he had not yet begun to rationalize or understand. His intuitive response nevertheless presaged a new era in which painting, delivered at last from its subjection to the world of external objects, would exist only in terms of itself, rooted in the power 'of forms, lines and colours assembled in a certain order'.

That prophetic description offered by Maurice Denis (later to be woefully misinterpreted) could never have been written by Kandinsky: the point at which the leader of the French Symbolists ended, with a conclusion about a technical economy of means in painting, was precisely the point of departure for Kandinsky's own aesthetic programme – a process of justifying that 'assembly', imparting to it a felt or expressive content not reducible to a 'material' or mechanical technique.

In 1901, Kandinsky founded the Phalanx group of artists, based in Schwabing. The studios were not only a workplace, but also a forum for the study and encouragement of the 'new art'. Exhibitions were organized that featured the works of Monet, Signac and Kublin. Although the traditional subjects were taught, the curriculum emphasized 'plein air' painting and modelling – both regarded as radical innovations. The Phalanx group did not survive for very long, and in 1904 Kandinsky closed down the school. But short-lived though it was, and probably highly disorganized, it was a remarkable experiment; it is also the first indication we have that Kandinsky was not content to be merely an artist. In fact, as we shall see, he placed great value on his role as an organizer and a teacher. Perhaps this is to be ascribed, at least in part, to a lingering messianic tradition of art, founded in the Romantic credo that the artist was the apostle of a superior

world of visions, feelings and ideas, accessible through art alone.

It was through the Phalanx group that Kandinsky met Gabriele Münter; initially his pupil, she soon became his intimate companion. During the next few years – from 1904 to 1908 – they travelled extensively together, first to Russia, then Holland, Tunisia, the French Riviera, and Rapallo, and also lived for a year in Paris, from June 1906 to June 1907; apparently Kandinsky was in the grip of some kind of neurotic compulsion to be always on the move. There can be little doubt that he was engaged on a personal quest, that he was dissatisfied with his previous activities, his attempts to try his hand, in quick succession, at Symbolism, the stylization of Art Nouveau (or Jugendstil, to use the German term), effects of formal simplication close to those of Neo-Impressionism, and the use of optical mixtures in the manner of Divisionism.

Whether or not he found any answers in the course of his incessant travels, he at least discovered that his work was beginning to attract attention abroad. He was asked to contribute to the Salon d'Automne and the Salon des Indépendants of 1903, and was a regular exhibitor thereafter. Opinions vary as to the significance of his time in Paris. On the whole he preferred to retreat to the peace and quiet of Sèvres rather than associate too closely with the bohemians of Montparnasse. His manner was stand-offish, if not actually unfriendly, and he showed little inclination to form any ties of friendship with the Parisian painters. Yet he took a close interest in Fauve painting, and Matisse in particular. He recognized in him concerns similar to his own: a desire to use violent colour to create an autonomous language of painting, an emphasis on the expressive power of the object that had the effect of rendering it practically unrecognizable. These were the influences that helped him to leave Symbolism behind and return once more to landscapes, and a direct confrontation with reality, with all the problems that implied.

The discovery of Murnau, in 1908, was an event of capital importance. Enchanted by the picturesque charm of this peaceful little town in the foothills of the Bavarian Alps, Kandinsky and Gabriele Münter decided to make it their home. They remained there for some years, using it as a base for intense periods of work, interspersed with trips to Munich. There was no danger of artistic isolation: Kandinsky's friend Jawlensky and Marianne von Werefkin were frequent visitors, and shared in communal painting sessions.

It was in Murnau that Kandinsky moved decisively away from the representation of the object towards an art totally liberated from figurative concerns. Of course, it was not a smooth progression, there were many hesitations and doubts, as well as a great deal of mental anguish. 'A terrible abyss,' he wrote, 'a flood of questions of all kinds welled up in me, concerning my responsibilities. The most important being: what is to replace the missing object?'

It would be wrong to regard the invention of abstraction as a purely formal development – that would be to deny the fantastic conceptual effort involved in such a radical departure – but, that said, the inexorable advance of abstraction can be traced through the series of landscapes painted at this time, which show a progressive reduction of figurative motifs.

The first pictures painted in Murnau are striking for the extraordinary luminosity of their colours, with a preference for violent oppositions of complementary blues and yellows, a vibrant chromatic intensity that blurs the precision of the construction. Gradually the forms become more simplified, more stylized, until eventually they are no more than structures, or 'signs' (triangles, diagonals, arcs), with only the most glacing contact with reality.

Kandinsky was a tireless initiator, and in 1909 he founded a new group, the New Artists' Association of Munich (NKV), his intention being to inject some life into a prevailing apathy and, once again, to propagate his own ideas and beliefs. The manifesto of the Association, which must have been written by Kandinsky, states quite explicitly: 'We start out from the idea that the artist, over and above the impressions he receives from the external world, from Nature, also at all times experiences the tumultuous activity of his inner world . . . the search for forms free of all superfluity and capable of expressing the essential, the hope for an artistic synthesis, that is our watchword, which commands the support of a growing number of artists . . .'

The Association organized conferences and exhibitions and also issued publications. In 1910, an international exhibition was held that included works by Braque, Picasso, Derain and Vlaminck, among others. Although the Munich critics were bitterly hostile, the display captivated the young Franz Marc, who immediately joined the Association. When conflicts arose in the group – perhaps because of jealousy – Kandinsky and Marc found themselves alone, isolated from the others, who openly condemned them for the extravagance of their ideas.

But Kandinsky and Marc were undeterred. The conviction that they were on the way to discovering the truth, reinforced by mutual friendship and respect, encouraged them to persevere in the defence of their art. So the Blaue Reiter was born, first in the form of the famous almanac that bears that name, designed to be an annual anthology of articles and reviews, accompanied by original and photographic illustrations – 'a book-mirror that will establish links with the past and project a ray of light into the future' was how Kandinsky described it. The significance of the curious title has been much discussed. It arose in fact as an item of 'personal mythology', one of those word associations that becomes a private reference, more like a secret code than an explicit description. On one occasion Kandinsky explained, with breathtaking ingenuousness: '... We both liked blue, Marc liked horses, I liked riders ...'

There can be no doubt that the sky-blue figure of the rider also had a symbolic significance in the minds of the two men: it represented departure towards a destination, energy directed towards an end. The Blaue Reiter was a phenomenon of considerable importance. In the one volume of the almanac ever published, and in the two exhibitions, were included some of the most interesting writings and paintings of those pre-war years, virtually a résumé of the international artistic scene, with commentaries provided by the leading members of the avant-garde. In the contents list of the almanac one reads such names as Burliuk, Macke and Schoenberg, alongside those of Marc and, of course, Kandinsky, who published in it not only his essay 'On the Question of Form' (a first treatment of the ideas contained in *Concerning the Spiritual in Art and Painting in Particular*, printed in late 1911), but also two ventures in 'artistic synthesis' – an article 'Concerning theatrical composition' and *Yellow Sound*, a scenario for a total spectacle (not actually performed until 1976).

The activities of the Blaeu Reiter made Munich one of the foremost centres of the European avant-garde, and assured the members of the group a growing reputation.

It was at this time that Herwarth Walden, a towering personality of the Berlin intelligentsia, opened his gallery Der Sturm. It took its name from the review of which he was editor, and which was committed to defending the new art against 'everything that is decayed, bourgeois and out of date'. Following an exhibition held by the artists of the Blaue Reiter, Walden invited Kandinsky to present a retrospective of his work, in September 1912. Kandinsky's first one-man show comprised 72 works dating from 1902 to 1912, and was accompanied by a

major catalogue composed largely of texts written by the painter. Walden was delighted: in fact he was so impressed that he asked Kandinsky and Marc to help him set up a German version of the Salon d'Automne. Kandinsky was given responsibility for selecting the Russian artists; he made an eclectic choice, illustrating all the most modern tendencies. Walden, as part of his continuing effort to promote Kandinsky's painting, undertook to publish an album containing 67 reproductions of the artist's work. It was a major project, and had to be negotiated with great delicacy since Kandinsky's views were often at variance with his publisher's, but, sadly, it never came to fruition; war was declared on 1 August 1914, as printing was about to start.

In parallel with his activities in Berlin, Kandinsky published his treatise *Concerning the Spiritual in Art*, a work of startling originality in terms both of style and content. The idea of abstraction was not in itself new, but Kandinsky showed it in an entirely fresh perspective. Inevitably, there has been much debate as to the sources that may have influenced him.

An indispensable contemporary work of reference was Wilhelm Worringer's *Abstraktion und Einfühlung* (*Abstraction and Intuition*). Published in Munich in 1907, the book undoubtedly provided a powerful stimulus to German artists. In it the author discusses the drive towards 'abstraction experienced in all the arts, part of a bi-polarity between Realism and the Abstract'. The emphasis is on the primacy of the search for the Essential as an indispensable part of every creative act, even though times and fashions may change, manifesting itself in an intuitive attempt to develop a new means of codification.

Although it is tempting to make a link between this study and the conclusions put forward by Kandinsky, the analogy does not in fact stand up to examination. First, Worringer, like the German comparative school of the

Kandinsky and Nina
in Munich in 1913

Kandinsky and Nina in 1925

Kandinsky and Nina in Hendaye, 1929

Kandinsky and Schönberg with their wives in 1927

time, relies on an iconographical analysis, confining himself strictly to a study of the stylistic evolution of forms. Even more important, there is every reason to believe that Kandinsky was not aware of the book until as late as 1910, when he heard about it from Franz Marc, at a time when the evidence of his own writing and painting confirms he was already committed to abandoning figuration. Finally, and crucially, where Worringer, and to a degree Bergson, treat intuition as the product of a particular attitude – something like Picasso's reliance on the workings of serendipity – Kandinsky believes in the pre-existence of a Pantheon of a cosmic order, to which the work of art attempts to respond with a comparable expression in its own language. It is an eschatalogical view of art, substantially different not only from the pragmatic interpretation advanced by Worringer, but also from the various other aesthetic theories with which Kandinsky was later to cross swords.

Perhaps we should not therefore be surprised to find that it is theosophy, and the teachings of Rudolf Steiner, that are the major influence and reference point in the argument presented in *Concerning the Spiritual*? Its central thesis is that the topic of spirituality, characterized by its universality and liberation, is the only possible source of inspiration for the artist, who should therefore commit himself to an 'antimaterialism' (or an 'immaterialism') that is accessible to all. The system of reference is the musical language, which Kandinsky sees as the most apt metaphor for 'describing' the new pictorial syntax that is dedicated to combating material contingencies, a task beyond the scope of the traditional language of art. Uniting theory with practice, in that same year (1911) Kandinsky embarked on his series of *Improvisations, Impressions* and *Compositions*.

Kandinsky drew an explicit distinction between the three 'modes': the 'impressions' were still to be related to the shock to the emotions experienced on regarding the spectacle of nature; the 'improvisations' were the expression of inner, unconscious nature; the 'compositions' were attempts to achieve a synthesis entirely unrelated to external contingency, paintings of extreme asceticism, in which the artist was guided solely by 'inner necessity' – achieved with difficulty and only after a long process of elaboration, founded in 'clear consciousness of intention and adaptation to reality' – the final product being something which Kandinsky compared to 'polyphony'. The three definitions encapsulate the transition from figurative to abstract. The 'objective' subject of painting transforms itself by degrees into the 'subjective' subject of its creator, whose task is to extract from the form (or line) 'the pure inner sonority'. All the elements he uses are governed by a common principle of equivalence, whatever their outward appearance: 'it is a matter of total indifference whether an artist uses a real or an abstract form, for, within themselves, these two forms are identical [as long as their] inner sonority has not been weakened by any secondary role and reveals itself with its full force', maintained Kandinsky.

In this statement lies the explanation for the coexistence in Kandinsky's *oeuvre*, during this short pre-war period, of purely abstract works with those still retaining narrative elements.

It is a truth that does much to temper the arrogant, iconoclastic image of Kandinsky presented by uncomprehending critics, bitterly hostile to a form of painting they regarded as completely detached from reality. Kandinsky was never a fanatic, and it would be both wrong and a gross over-simplification to ascribe to him the full weight of responsibility for abandoning reality in favour of pure plastic construction. His own hesitations and doubts reflect his consciousness of the gravity of taking such an irrevocable step. They are proof both of his personal modesty and of the traumatic nature of these events for him.

MOSCOW, REVOLUTION AND PAINTING

Kandinsky arrived in Moscow in December 1914, preceded by his reputation as a highly respected and innovative artist. By the time he left Russia for good, in December 1921, having been sent on an official mission to Germany, circumstances had altered dramatically. His ideas provoked fierce opposition, and his attitudes were criticized for being out of date.

It was a period in Kandinsky's life which many of his biographers, following Grohmann, have described as 'transitional'; as the land of the Czars was transformed into the seething hotbed of activity that was the Soviet Republic, the Russian painter found himself in a paradoxical situation, prey to doubts and indecisions that had a profoundly inhibiting effect.

Aside from a number of pictures that re-introduced elements of figuration, characteristic of this 'Russian period', Kandinsky produced very little in the way of actual painting; he saw abstract art developing on lines that he found unacceptable, and felt bound to state his opposition in whatever way was open to him. His teaching appointment provided him with the opportunity to experiment with the pedagogical methods he later developed at the Bauhaus, and his constant questioning of his own art laid the foundations for the theoretical arguments of *Point and Line to Plane*.

Long afterwards he declared 'they were years I prefer to forget.' Yet it is clear, if only because he needed to make the remark at all, that he could not forget them; bitterness was mingled with nostalgia for his homeland.

Profoundly convinced that 'the matter of art is beyond Time', he found himself plunged into an atmosphere where politics dominated every sphere of activity; accus-

tomed to the comforts of life, he was appalled to experience financial hardship. Then, too, there was his separation from Gabriele Münter, who left for Stockholm in 1916, and the report in the same year of the death of his friend Franz Marc on the battle front at Verdun. Kandinsky found himself in an emotional desert, a situation only partly remedied by his relationship with Nina Andreevskaia, whom he married in 1917.

His profound unhappiness during these years has generally been attributed to his feelings of alienation, the sense of being virtually an ex-patriate in his own country.

As an explanation it is hardly satisfactory. Kandinsky had always maintained his contacts with Russia and returned there on frequent visits. From 1903 onwards he had exhibited regularly in Odessa, Moscow and St Petersburg. He even invited artists from Moscow to participate in the activities of the Blaue Reiter. In addition, his writings and paintings were known to a wide audience and were much discussed. A message from Kandinsky was read out to the Congress of Russian Artists of 1912 (it was a summary of the argument of *Concerning the Spiritual*). He was also a member of the Knave of Diamonds group, and took part, with other representatives of the international avant-garde, in two polemical exhibitions held in 1911 and 1912.

The other reasons for his discontent are largely 'historical', or due to an accident of the generations. In spite of the difference in their ages, Kandinsky was contemporary with Larionov, Goncharova, and David and Kasimir Burliuk. These artists had already evolved a mature style and established their reputations by the time a second generation emerged, among them Malevich, Tatlin, Rodchenko, Pevsner, Gabo and Lissitzky . . . They were the true ideologues of artistic materialism, with their Constructivist and Positivist movements. It was they who challenged the established painters in a debate that was

Kandinsky with members of the Narkompros

not only about their different views of the social functions of art, but also about problems of aesthetics; the art of Larionov, Goncharova and Kandinsky was condemned as being hopelessly out of tune with the times.

They bore the brunt of the attack, launched as part of a systematic campaign to destroy their moral authority and reduce their influence in society, along with that of the aesthetic philosophy they espoused. Larionov and Goncharova chose the course of exile, and went to Paris to join Diaghilev and the Ballets Russes company. Kandinsky decided to stay behind and fight a tactical battle, accepting the opportunity, when it was offered to him, to play a part in the process of reform instituted at every level of the youthful Republic.

Thus there is no real justification for claiming that Kandinsky felt alienated, a stranger in his own country. On the contrary, it was because he regarded himself as Russian, and was regarded by others as Russian, that he became so embroiled in the ideological debates of the day, to the point of accepting a state appointment, where he could use his position to make clear his opposition to total revolution and cultural upheaval – and this in spite of the fact that he himself, whether he liked it or not, was already identified with the mistakes of the past.

Kandinsky was certainly not a revolutionary; in 1917 he was content to observe the dramatic events of the October uprising without becoming involved. Nor was he a reactionary, in the sense of being a typical turn-of-the-century Russian aristocrat. Yet he did not hide his élitist sympathies, which he expounded at some length in *Concerning the Spiritual in Art*, using the metaphor of the 'spiritual triangle', a kind of pyramid with the elect at the top. Although Kandinsky was concerned solely with cultural considerations, which bore no direct relationship to the structure of society, it was inevitable that such ideas, deriving from a pragmatic and intuitive response to

reality, would annoy the Constructivists. They regarded culture as a product of society, subordinate to it, and having as its function to imagine practical solutions that accorded with a belief in materialism.

To the inventor of the 'principle of inner necessity', an intrinsically materialistic art was anathema. It was not long before a state of permanent warfare existed between Kandinsky and the Constructivist leaders, Rodchenko and Lissitzky, while at the same time there was a series of violent exchanges with Malevich, which never quite amounted to a complete breakdown of relations.

Indeed, a comparative study of the works of Malevich and Kandinsky reveals more than a few points of similarity. Suprematism had a metaphysical basis. 'By Suprematism I understand the supremacy of feeling or of pure sensation in the pictorial arts,' wrote Malevich in the introduction to the Suprematist manifesto, using terms that Kandinsky himself would not have repudiated.

Their aesthetic systems were comparable in several respects: 'In 1913,' Malevich continued, 'when I was struggling desperately to liberate art from that ballast that is the world of objects, I found my salvation in the form of the *Square* . . . It was not a simple empty square that I exhibited, rather it was *the experience of the absence of the object.*'

Both arrived at about the same time (1917–20) at similar accounts of the properties of the 'surface-plane' (or as Kandinsky described it rather more fancifully, the 'original plane'); the flat-coloured figures of squares and trapeziums in the Suprematist pictures are the exact counterparts of Kandinsky's 'ovals', 'circles' and 'pictures-within-the-picture'. While Malevich proceeded by conducting a logical investigation of the physical properties of the picture, Kandinsky reached very similar solutions via a seemingly more intuitive response to the resonance of forms and colours.

Kandinsky's experiments, while in Moscow, with this kind of purely geometric abstraction were limited in their scope, but were to bear fruit in his later work with the Bauhaus. There is every reason to believe that he was very interested in the Suprematist principles of pictorial construction. He must have been impressed by the speed with which Malevich moved towards the liberation of form from its representative function, and can hardly have been indifferent to his introduction of a 'fourth dimension' (the time-element he himself emphasized), as a function of the potential movement of forms.

Where the two approaches differed, however, was in their opposing conceptions of the artists's role: Malevich's ideal of the 'proletarian artist' was poles apart from the reality represented by Kandinsky, that of the 'creative artist'.

Nevertheless, it was a time when every resource available was directed towards the establishment of a socialist state. Lenin and Trotsky believed in the social efficacy of art, and supported the enlistment of artists and intellectuals in an active cultural campaign. In 1918, on Tatlin's recommendation, Kandinsky was asked to join the People's Commissariat for Education (Narkompros), and was appointed to the staff of the Vkhutemos (the Moscow Free Art Studios). A year later he was put in charge of reorganizing 22 provincial museums, and was then made director of the newly-founded Museum of Pictorial Culture, with responsibility for the acquisition of new works; he took the opportunity to purchase numerous abstract paintings, among them thirty or so of his own.

In 1920 his pedagogical abilities were again pressed into service, and he was given overall charge of the curriculum of INKHUK (the Institute of Artistic Culture). Kandinsky proposed to make the basis of the teaching programme a study of the interaction of the different art forms, with particular concentration on a comparative study of music and painting. His plans, which reflected his own theories on the correspondence between the rules of musical composition and the relationships of line and colour, were judged unacceptable by the representatives of Constructivism. To them it seemed clear that the desirable synthesis was not that which could be realized between the different artistic disciplines but rather a co-operation between art and industry, with a bias towards technical applications.

Kandinsky was in a minority and unable to implement the programme of artistic education he had devised. Disappointed, and increasingly under attack from Rodchenko and Lissitzky, he resigned from INKHUK.

His nomination as vice-president of the Academy of Artistic Sciences, established in June 1921, represented his last attempt to work within the new structure of society, which he had come to judge more and more severely. Kandinsky's problem was that he was, quite literally, an anachronism: his belief in a 'spiritual component' was ill-received and largely misunderstood, he himself was out of step with the doctrines and dogmas of revolution, and amid universal proclamations of 'liberation', he found his own freedom of action severely curtailed.

When he left for Berlin, on an official visit to study the operations of the Bauhaus, he had no idea that he was soon to become a part of that organization, and would come to be regarded as one of its most eminent members. If he was resigned to leaving Russia, it was not for want of trying to play his part in the establishment of a democratic socialist society. Subsequent events go a long way towards justifying his position: the seizure of power by Stalin brought to an end a period of enthusiastic experiment which, Nina Kandinsky was to say, was 'benevolent and favourable to creativity and the artistic avant-garde.' It was replaced by repression and reaction, which led inevitably to the extinction of all worthwhile cultural activity.

KANDINSKY AT THE BAUHAUS
ART, DECORATION, TEACHING

Back in Berlin, Nina and Vassily Kandinsky were at first dazzled by the richness of the intellectual life. During the twenties, the German capital was home to some of the finest minds of the artistic and scientific avant-garde.

But Kandinsky was upset by the change of environment. In the year he spent in Berlin he painted only two pictures. He delivered a few lectures, but on the whole did not involve himself in the quarrels between the Dadaists and the Neo-Realists of the Neue Sachlichkeit. He also seemed indifferent to the ripples created by the growing Symbolist movement and to the Neo-Plasticism of Mondrian and van Doesburg.

In March 1922, Walter Gropius and Alma Mahler invited Kandinsky to teach at the Bauhaus. He accepted their proposal with relief, chiefly motivated, if we are to believe his wife Nina, by the hope that Weimar would offer him a peaceful and ordered existence, allowing him to concentrate on his painting.

According to Kandinsky himself, the reality was rather different. He confided to Schoenberg that he found it difficult to reconcile his 'teaching activities, the communal life imposed by the rules of the school, and [his] own work.' His criticisms may, however, be somewhat exaggerated, since there is every evidence that – after an initial period of familiarization – he felt very much at home with the emphasis on experimental teaching methods, and also found kindred spirits and good friends in Paul Klee and Lionel Feininger. Above all, as he declared with some pride, he was respected and understood. Certainly the rapid progress of his work, and his readiness to carry abstraction into hitherto unexplored areas, suggest a mind at peace with itself. How else, given his many other responsibilities, could he have completed his major work *Point and Line to Plane*, which set out the theoretical basis of his teaching?

To what extent Kandinsky put his personal stamp on the successive Bauhaus curricula is hard to say, since the programme was not founded on a single, coherent artistic philosophy, in fact rather the reverse. The school was unusual in that everyone had the right to express a view, for Gropius believed, with some justification, that dissent and debate created a dynamic of their own, setting up a permanent dialectic. This approach to teaching was enshrined in the Bauhaus manifesto, issued by Gropius in 1919, and which proposed: '. . . a synthesis of the fine arts and the minor arts and crafts . . . with the intention of basing teaching not on imitation but on creativity.' The role of the teaching staff was to reveal the properties of materials and forms through direct experiment, and to awaken and stimulate the creative talents of the pupils.

It was a programme Kandinsky could hardly fault, since it broadly resembled the proposals he had put forward for INKHUK, designed to 'create men of vision.' The terminology is slightly different, but it seems likely that Gropius's motivation was not so very different from Kandinsky's own.

The first Bauhaus, based in Weimar, was centred around artists rather than practitioners. By a curious omission, Gropius was the only architect. As he gradually came to realize that this accorded ill with the declared aims of the school, he embarked on a series of reforms to give the Bauhaus a new direction, summed up in the rallying call: 'Art and Technology, a new Unity.' This explicit linking of art and industry was to have far-reaching consequences. First, came the resignation, amid much protestation, of Johannes Itten, a proponent of 'art for art's sake', who believed in the primacy of the individual artist's role and

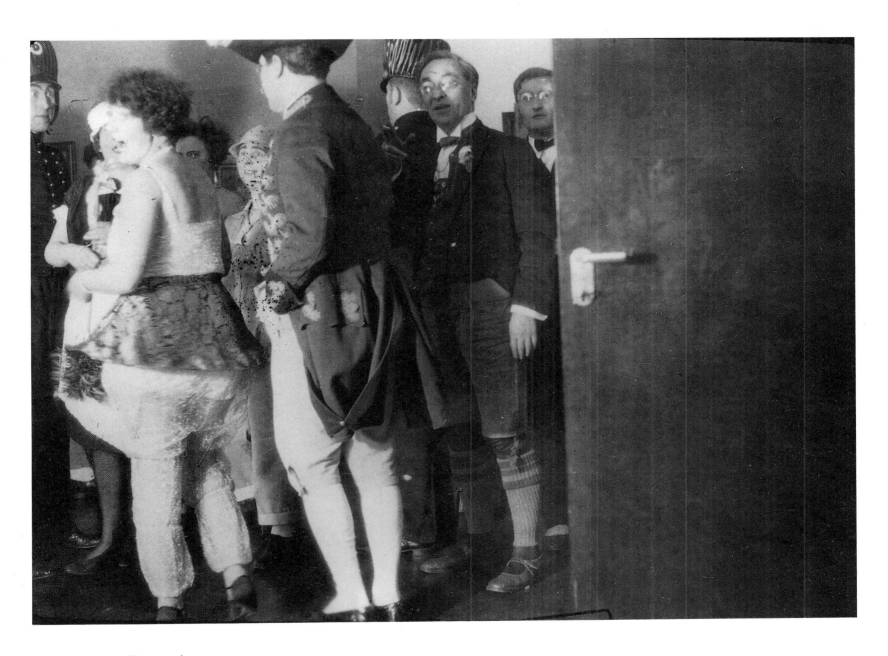

Celebration in Dessau in 1928

Kandinsky, Gropius and Oud in Weimar in 1923
Group of Bauhaus academics in Dessau in 1926

resisted the subordination of art to technology. Then there was a change in the whole basis of the teaching; the original bias towards creativity and intuition was replaced by an emphasis on 'constructivist' and technological research. The 'stimulation of creativity' gave way to an overriding insistence that 'function determined form.' Artists were replaced by pragmatists. The main burden of the teaching was handed over to the younger generation, Albers, Breuer and Bayer, themselves trained at the Bauhaus.

Although Gropius's 'liberalism' gave scope for the artists to continue with their own work, without pressure to conform to the new philosophy, there could well have been a problem for established personalities like Feininger, Klee and Kandinsky in coming to terms with a new *status quo*, where their own influence was much diminished. The fact is, they not only adapted surprisingly well, they had already anticipated what would happen and laid their plans accordingly, demonstrating an acute awareness of the situation. On their insistence, they were put in charge of 'free' painting studios, attendance at which formed an element of the basic curriculum, and they also participated directly in the construction of the prototypes produced at the Bauhaus.

It was at this time that Kandinsky chose to examine one possible future orientation for the art of abstraction, namely, its decorative function, or integration within the 'decorative arts'. Kandinsky devised a sort of logical equation: '. . . if decorative art is "beautiful", and it has within it sufficient spirituality, then its diffusion will allow the greatest possible number to have access to spirituality.' This belief in a process of 'contamination', designed to make art available to all, was a central proposition of the original 'Arts and Crafts' movement in Victorian England; its influence was widespread and manifested itself abroad in various different guises, *inter alia* in the *Werkbund*

founded by van de Velde, the immediate precursor of the Bauhaus, which concerned itself in particular with methods of industrial production.

Kandinsky's espousal of such notions is remarkable, not so much for his acceptance of a proselytizing role for art – although one remembers his metaphor of the pyramid accessible only to the elect – as for the original slant he introduced into what was essentially a social ideal. Of course decorative art existed, in its many forms, but it could truly serve its purpose only if *function* were the product of 'inner necessity', and *form* had its 'proper sonority'; only then would it constitute 'a first step towards the recognition of pure spirituality.' Or, to put in another way, Kandinsky stressed that it was the task of the Creator alone to disseminate 'beauty', and it was

Kandinsky and Klee imitating the monument
to Goethe and Schiller in 1929

inconceivable that he could serve a lesser 'beauty' that was no more than an ephemeral reflection of 'taste'.

It was not by chance then that, during this period, Kandinsky became interested in the whole idea of 'kitsch' objects, and that his own painting made use of series of repeated forms, exploring the facility offered by stylistic effects, and examining the decorative properties of forms through the precise use of the decorative motifs then in fashion.

This geometric idiom of squares, diamonds, circles, grids, lines and entwined curves has considerable charm and compositional elegance; on a superficial level at least, the obvious comparison is with Art Deco, much applauded at the World Fair held in Paris in 1925.

The Bauhaus years also presented Kandinsky with the

opportunity to extend his contacts with the United States. Although his work was already known there, from the time of the Armory Show of 1913, he was subsequently indebted to the efforts on his behalf of Katherine S. Dreier. She was a fanatical devotee of contemporary art and co-founder, with Man Ray and Marcel Duchamp, of the Société Anonyme, of which Kandinsky was elected vice-president in 1923. Miss Dreier organized travelling exhibitions of the works of Malevich, Mondrian, Duchamp, Brancusi and Kandinsky, and it was through her that Solomon Guggenheim was introduced to Kandinsky's painting, becoming ultimately one of his most enthusiastic collectors. She also made strenuous efforts to have an English translation made of *Point and Line to Plane*, published in 1926 as the ninth in a series of *Bauhausbücher*.

Kandinsky was working on the ideas contained in the book as early as 1914. The notes he made then, with corrections added at the time he was giving lectures in Berlin, were finally assembled in a form ready for publication in 1925, when the Bauhaus had just moved from Weimar to Dessau and all those involved were waiting for the new buildings to be completed.

Point and Line to Plane set out to expound a 'pedagogical method', being a systematic account of Kandinsky's ideas on the expressive possibilities of the basic elements of painting. In fact it went far beyond that, emerging in its final form as a comprehensive theory of abstraction, defining the laws of 'non-objective' composition.

Although the first section of the book consists in a number of intuitive insights, the second is devoted to the attempt to establish 'a methodical vocabulary of all the words [or, plastic elements] currently stripped and deprived of their meaning.' There are frequent references to the natural sciences and technology, and parallels have also been detected with contemporary researches into Gestalt psychology, in particular studies on the nature of perception. Yet it has now been established with absolute certainty that Kandinsky was not aware of the work being done in that field. One may regret that he did not keep abreast of the latest developments in psychology – or indeed in materialist or phenomenological philosophy – but his ignorance in these respects is hardly surprising. Although *Point and Line to Plane* borrows from scientific method, Kandinsky was not an academic, and he never sought to acquire knowledge beyond what he thought would be useful for his particular concerns. His scholarship was strictly limited, and he operated in general by a process of intuitive insights, analogies and affinities. The book does not set out to be a scientifically verifiable thesis, but rather represents an ambitious – and hugely rewarding – attempt to codify the types of plastic expression. Obviously Kandinsky knew he was, in a sense, attempting the impossible – since visual phenomena cannot, ultimately, be reduced to a syntactical order – but the book is a quite remarkable piece of work and an indispensable record, the product of the period of history when 'non-objective' art was obliged to present its credentials, and stand up and take its place in the company of the more dominant strands of Neo-Impressionism and Expressionism; in giving voice to the logic of the development of abstraction, the book at the same time reveals its origins as an emotional response to exclusion by Constructivist tendencies.

In the Germany of the thirties, the rise of Nazism seemed to be unstoppable. The Bauhaus school had already been forced to move from Weimar to Dessau, and in 1933 it finally closed its doors. The particular form of intolerance that prevailed in Germany at that time forced many intellectuals into exile. Most of the Bauhaus teachers emigrated to the United States, but Kandinsky, in spite of invitations to go with them, determined to settle in Paris, where he believed the atmosphere was likely to be particularly conducive to the practice of art.

PARIS AND THE LATE PAINTINGS

At the suggestion of Marcel Duchamp, Kandinsky and his wife Nina made their home in Neuilly, in a block of flats newly constructed on the banks of the Seine.

Biographers have tended to be less than forthcoming over the last eleven years of Kandinsky's life, his 'Paris period'. It is as though they prefer to draw a veil over the late paintings – regarded as at best disconcerting and at worst appalling – in order not to tarnish the image of the great master of abstract art.

The full explanation for this reticence turns out to be more complicated, and it is only very recently that serious research has been undertaken, which throws light on the background to what amounts to a conspiracy of silence.

It would be no exaggeration to say that Kandinsky's relations with the artistic establishment in France were characterized by mutual misunderstanding. When he arrived in Paris, Kandinsky believed his exile was a purely temporary expedient, and declared his willingness to return to Germany immediately there were signs of an improvement.

He persisted in this attitude and, even though examples of his work were featured in the sinister exhibition of 'degenerate art' mounted by the Nazis, he nevertheless attempted to make a pact with the devil, by sending a letter to the authorities in Berlin reminding them 'that he had lived most of his life in Germany, was a German citizen and was only in Paris for reasons of his art.'

Although he himself refused to be identified with French society, he nevertheless could not understand why the major dealers, such as Kahnweiler or Rosenberg, showed no interest in his paintings. His disappointment was compounded by the discovery that his work was barely known at all in Paris. It must be said that his situation was not unique. Paris prided itself on being the artistic capital of the world and there was a fundamental lack of interest in

Kandinsky
in 1936

anything that happened on the fringes of its empire. There were those who tried to help him – encouraging him to take a part in the factional squabbles among artists that are the peculiar charm of 'Parisian life'. Breton extended a warm welcome and invited him to join the Surrealists. Kandinsky was evasive, and then refused. He found Surrealism too politicized, too erotic and too populist in its concerns. Breton responded by accusing Kandinsky of being a reactionary, and condemning his equivocal attitude towards Nazism and Mussolini's Italy.

Christian Zervos, the publisher and art dealer, organized two exhibitions of Kandinsky's work, and also asked him to contribute to the *Cahiers d'Art*. Once again there was a disagreement, apparently because Zervos had been in part responsible for an exhibition at the Petit Palais which, out of a sort of reflex nationalism, attempted to show that Cubism was the origin of all abstract art. There can be no doubt that Kandinsky was a prickly character, that he was arrogant in his manner and difficult to deal with, but not everyone found it impossible to work with him. Tériade commissioned some illustrations for *Verve*, San Lazzaro, who was a devotee of his work, founded the review *XXe Siècle* at his suggestion, and devoted a whole issue to Kandinsky's painting. And Jeanne Bucher, the director of a small avant-garde gallery, agreed to provide a regular showplace for his work; in 1942, while Paris was occupied, they collaborated on the last exhibition of Kandinsky's work held during his lifetime.

Kandinsky still felt misunderstood, ill at ease in a society that failed to accept him at his true worth. He retreated to Neuilly and his visits to Paris became increasingly infrequent. Yet he was not isolated; whether his contemporaries liked it or not, younger artists admired him and offered their friendship. Miró, Magnelli, Arp and Sophie Tauber were regular visitors to the studio flat at Neuilly. There were obvious affinities between them: Hans Arp's soft geometry, Miró and Magnelli's figures floating in indeterminate space, had much in common with the organic shapes Kandinsky was painting during this period. It is this that has been the principal charge against Kandinsky in his latter years, not so much that he radically altered his style, abandoning the strict geometry of his last Bauhaus works, as that he reintroduced into his work an element of figuration, in the form of animal and vegetable 'organisms' decked out in fantastic colour schemes that have been judged tasteless.

It is an image of Kandinsky that has done his reputation much harm, especially as he never disguised the sheer personal pleasure he derived from painting in this manner. Undoubtedly many people were annoyed and angry at his assumed nonchalance, which they regarded as a deliberate blindness to all that was going on in France at that time. But once again, it is not the whole truth. Certainly he was no longer the inspired Kandinsky of the pre-war years in Munich, but he retained a sharp awareness of the most modern tendencies of the avant-garde. Judged as compositions, or by their choice of themes, his last paintings are quite as ambitious as anything that Neo-Futurism or 'art concret' was able to offer, and his investigations of materials (sand paintings, industrial paintings, etc.) are of striking modernity. At the same time he continued his researches into the 'original plane', as it related to the figure. The space in which his forms are set is not so much space without depth as space that is empty. The liberation of the surface plane is the only way of destroying the illusion of materiality; Kandinsky's 'figures' cling to this surface, refusing to take their place in any hierarchy of successive planes that would be suggestive of a third dimension.

Even if it was now peopled with invented creatures and half-familiar grotesques, Kandinsky's was still an 'immaterial' world.

Sounds (Klänge)
Poems by Kandinsky

The following four poems are from *Sounds (Klänge)*, a collection that Kandinsky published in Munich in 1912, in German, in a limited edition accompanied by wood engravings in black and in colour.

I – Some Things

A fish went plunging into the water. He was silver. The water blue. I tracked him with my eyes. The fish went deeper down. But I still saw him. I saw him again when I could see him no more.

Yes, yes, I saw the fish. Yes, yes, I saw him. I saw him. I saw him. I saw him. I saw him. I saw him. I saw him.

A white horse stood quietly on his long legs. The sky was blue. His legs were long. The horse was motionless. His mane hung down and did not stir. The horse stayed motionless on his long legs. But he was alive. Not a quiver of a muscle. Not a twitch of his hide. He was alive.

Yes, yes, he was alive.

On the open field a flower grew. The flower was blue. There was only one flower on the open field.

Yes, yes, it was there.

II – In the Forest

The forest was becoming denser and denser. The red trunks thicker and thicker. The green crowns heavier and heavier. The air darker and darker. The undergrowth more and more tangled. The toadstools more and more numerous. In the end you had to walk on all the toadstools. The man found it harder and harder to walk, to force a path, not to slip. But he did it, and repeated faster and faster the same phrase over and over again:

> The scars that heal
> The colours that correspond

To his left and a little behind walked a woman. Each time the man finished the phrase, she said in a very earnest way, rolling her 'r's very distinctly: verrry prrractical.

III – Leaves

I can remember one thing.

A very large black triangular mountain reached up to the sky. Its silvery summit was barely visible. To the right of this mountain was a very thick tree, its crown very bushy. This crown was so bushy that you could not distinguish the individual leaves. To the left and in one place only, but very thickly, there grew little white flowers which looked like little flat plates.

Apart from that, nothing.

I was standing in front of this landscape and looking.

All at once a man arrived on the right. Riding on a white goat, quite ordinary-looking except its horns stuck forward instead of back. And its tail, instead of pointing up as usual, hung down and was bald.

The man, on the other hand, had a blue face and a little snub nose. He was laughing and showing his small well-spaced teeth, worn but very white. I also noticed something bright red. He passed by slowly on his goat and disappeared behind the mountain.

What was strange was that when I looked back to the landscape, all the leaves had fallen to the ground and to the left there were no more flowers. Nothing but red berries.

True the mountain had not moved.

Not that time.

IV – Brightly Coloured Field

On a field where there was no grass but only flowers of all colours, five men were sitting in a row. A sixth was standing, to one side. The first said:

'The roof is safe . . . It's safe, the roof . . . Safe . . .'

After a moment, the second said:

'Don't touch me: I'm sweating . . . Sweating's what I'm doing . . . Yes!'

Then the third:

'Not over the wall!

Not over the wall! No!'

But the fourth:

'Ripening fruit!'

After a long pause, the fifth cried in a piercing voice:

'Wake him! Open wide his eyes! A stone is rolling down the mountain! A stone, a stone, a stone! A stone!! . . . Off the mountain! . . . It's rolling at us! . . . Open wide his ears! Oh, open wide his eyes! Give him long legs! Long, long . . . legs!!'

The sixth who was standing to one side let out a loud, brief cry:

'Silence!'

Old Town II, *1902*
Oils on canvas, 52 × 78.5 cm

While he was living in Munich, Kandinsky liked to go out and explore the Bavarian countryside, one of its attractions being 'those villages that have something very strange and distinctive about them'.

This view of Rothenburg ob der Tauber is a particularly interesting example. Attracted by the picturesque qualities of the medieval city, Kandinsky painted it in a style still very much influenced by Cézanne and the Post-Impressionists. The surfaces are simplified and there is too a hint of Divisionism in the handling; at the same time the shadows are made to appear quite disproportionate and mysterious, so that the scene has a strange atmosphere of frozen immobility. There were two versions of the picture, only the second of which survives. A painting called *Old Town*, which may have been a copy of the first state, was included by Kandinsky in a retrospective exhibition of his work, held at the Bern Kunsthalle in 1937.

Kandinsky's continuing affection for this particular canvas, its intrinsic qualities apart, was due in large measure to the nostalgia he felt for the landscapes of his youth.

Arab Town, 1905
Tempera on board, 67.3 × 99.5 cm

From December 1904 to April 1905, Kandinsky was in Tunisia with Gabriele Münter. He returned with a number of sketches executed *in situ* – rather more successful on this occasion than he had been when he visited Venice, in 1903, and was so enthralled by the magnificence of the place that he was unable to work at all: it was not until he was back in Germany that he embarked on a series of paintings, based on photographs taken by his companion. He followed much the same procedure with his studio paintings of the landscape and architecture of Tunisia, except that the sources he referred to were his own sketches.

Kandinsky always liked using tempera because of the clarity of the colours and the speed with which he could work. The 'arbitrary' colours and formal stylization of this painting are still reminiscent of the earlier Jugendstil compositions, but in its folk subject matter the work clearly anticipates the prints (engravings and woodcuts) he executed two years later, in Paris. The gouache was among the works shown by Kandinsky at the Salon d'Automne of 1905.

Park of St Cloud - with Horseman, 1906
Oils on board, 33 × 24cm

Of the series of ten small pictures executed in Sèvres, this work is of particular significance. It was one of the last oils painted by Kandinsky *en plein air* and, in terms of technique, betrays the influence of Signac and the Neo-Impressionists, even though the touch is rather broader and more incisive. Where it differs radically from Divisionism is in its freedom of interpretation and lack of concern for realistic detail: the emphasis is on effects of pure colour rather than an interplay of light and shade designed to suggest oppositions between forms.

Kandinsky seems already tempted to move away from 'the appearance of things', substituting the reality of vibrant chromatic intensity; it is a tentative step in the direction of Expressionism, looking forward to the style he was to develop in Murnau.

A final point of interest is the emblematic figure of the blue rider, a favourite motif of Kandinsky's, soon to be enshrined in symbolic form as the Blaue Reiter.

Autumn in Bavaria, 1908
Oils on board, 33 × 44.7cm

This view of a street in Murnau belongs with a group of paintings on a similar theme, all painted in the same year: *Murnau – Houses in the Obermarkt, Murnau Landscape, Houses in Murnau, Autumn* and *Winter No. 1*. With their schematic treatment of landscape, their bold design and brilliance of colour, they raise intriguing questions about the nature of Kandinsky's relationships with his contemporaries, and in particular the lessons he may have learned from his visits to avant-garde exhibitions in Paris and his participation in the Salon d'Automne. Apparently he preferred to spend his time in the solitude of his Sèvres apartment, and made no effort to meet the radical painters of the day. Yet he must have seen the Fauve paintings exhibited, with his, at the Salon, and cannot have been unaware of the major retrospectives of the works of Seurat, van Gogh and Cézanne. Although Kandinsky's personal contacts with other artists were very occasional, and certainly not solicited by him, the paintings of Derain, Matisse and Braque clearly influenced his palette. At the time when he himself was searching for an 'absolute painting', he can hardly have been indifferent to their heightened tones of pure colour and striking chromatic combinations, used, by Matisse in particular, as a means of achieving the autonomy of both colour and form.

Although Kandinsky refused to admit a direct influence, he did once write that 'the experience of foreign works' was beneficial, because it was 'similar to the experience of nature in its widest sense'.

Kandinsky's landscapes of towns and mountains, simplified in the extreme, are wonderfully harmonious displays of intense colour, and in this they are to be distinguished from the dramatic effects of the Expressionists and the extravagances of the Fauves.

The Blue Mountain, 1908-9
Oils on canvas, 106 × 96cm

Kandinsky moved to live in Murnau, a little village in Upper Bavaria, in a region of woods and valleys that he found captivating. The incessant travelling of the preceding years gave way to the peace and tranquillity of a settled life, punctuated only by occasional visits to Munich. At last he was ready to put his ideas onto canvas, setting them down in a great burst of activity; those years in Murnau (1908–14) have been described by Will Grohmann as a 'period of genius.' The determination with which Kandinsky pushed his ideas forward is truly astonishing, as is the speed with which he passed from painting that was still traditionally figurative to a highly disciplined abstraction.

The Blue Mountain is an excellent illustration of the transition. Although the subject is still visible, the handling and the relationships of colour have developed in an unexpected way. The diagonal touch, the flecking of pigment, the impasto, and above all the strident polarities of yellow and ultramarine, are the proof that the picture no longer relies for its coherence on conformity to external appearances. 'Objects lose their insistence,' Grohmann notes of this period. The themes tend generally towards fantasy, often representing purely imaginary scenes (the motif here is linked to the *Painting with Archer* in the Museum of Modern Art, New York). Grohmann detects as well a biblical influence, often apparent only in the choice of titles. There is too a persistent Symbolism, an influence Kandinsky found it difficult to shed, perhaps because he frequently worked with his friend Jawlensky, who had been deeply impressed by his encounter with the Nabis.

Improvisation 3, 1909
Oils on canvas, 94 × 130cm

With his series of *Improvisations*, *Impressions* and *Compositions*, Kandinsky introduces us into the world of signs and the dematerialization of form.

To make his intentions clear, he explains that the *Impressions* are pictures where he has started from nature and proceeded towards abstract forms; the *Improvisations* are spontaneous reactions to subjective experiences and emotions, and therefore derive from an inner compulsion; while the *Compositions* are more complex paintings, executed with painstaking precision, and arrived at only after numerous studies and sketches and preliminary drawings (see *Composition IV*). These titles, borrowed in the two latter cases from the vocabulary of music, reflect Kandinsky's desire to move in the direction of 'spiritual expression', enshrined in the 'principle of inner necessity.'

The series of *Improvisations* comprises, to our knowledge, 35 paintings, in contrast with only 6 *Impressions*. Often the *Improvisations* and *Impressions* were given a sub-title (*Impression IV* [*Gendarme*], for example), as though Kandinsky was still trying to retain some link with tangible reality – or perhaps, more accurately, because he found it difficult to make a final break with the external world, and abandon all last reference to the object.

The change was brought about gradually, and not without misgivings on Kandinsky's part. In this picture, recognizable objects are still present as the pretext for harmonies of colour and a dynamic linear structure; prominent in the centre of the composition, rearing up on its hind legs, is the already familiar figure of a blue horse.

Murnau - Landscape with Church II, 1910
Oils on canvas, 96.5 × 105.5 cm

A further illustration of Kandinsky's reluctance entirely to abandon figuration, this landscape is among the most 'expressionistic' he ever painted. Its links with the mainstream tradition of Expressionism are not so much a matter of the violent or exaggerated treatment of the subject, but of the resolute subjectivity of the handling. Naturalistic appearances are preserved, but metamorphosed and distorted by the operations of inner vision, which 'models reality, rather that taking it as its model'.

Today we have no problem in accepting a picture such as this; it has ceased to be regarded as shocking by a public accustomed to a tormented but still 'objective' view of reality. At the time it was painted, it caused a scandal. Shown, together with other even more 'abstract' works, at Kandinsky's first one-man exhibition, held at the Tannhauser gallery in 1911, it succeeded in outraging the Munich critics, who found it hard to accept such a profanation of the naturalistic ideal of Beauty. Curiously, the more purely abstract pictures escaped their wrath; either the critics chose to ignore them or, more probably, they simply failed to register their presence. The time had not yet come when abstraction was recognized as a part of painting.

Improvisation 10, 1910
Oils on canvas, 120 × 140cm

Although, in this painting, the forms themselves are no longer precisely stated, nevertheless the coloured masses are defined by black outlines, which serve to accentuate their distribution and the opposition between them, and to emphasize structure. In this process, the constituent elements of the whole gain in autonomy; there is no perceptible hierarchy according to which they are arranged or combined, and the resultant linear tensions occupy the whole of the surface area. Kandinsky thus succeeds both in escaping the traditional opposition between form and content, and in avoiding the illusion of perspective that would give prominence to the foreground. The circular, or spiral, composition, and the 'yellow triangle', are elements drawn from the vocabulary of forms and colours with spiritual resonance set out in *Concerning the Spiritual in Art*, on which Kandinsky was working at this time.

Improvisation 14, 1910
Oils on canvas, 74 × 125.5 cm

From preparatory studies for this painting (pencil and Indian ink drawings), we know that it represents a confrontation between two horsemen. Here there is nothing of graphic stillness and precision; rather Kandinsky is concerned to accentuate the dynamism of colour and line – in his own words, to make the picture 'a dynamic act', transposing the idea of motion into the pictorial expression itself.

In this picture the movement is one of convergence, centring on the impending impact between the two riders and their mounts. In *Improvisation 7* (now in the Tretiakov Gallery, Moscow) the movement is all directed upwards. But in both cases, it is by freeing the correspondence between line and colour, by treating the planes and coloured masses as imprecise entities, and by making them appear to slide across the surface of the canvas, that Kandinsky achieves his effect of instability and blurred motion – so radically different from the conventional vision of painting that he was accused by some critics of entering 'the abyss of pure pictorialism'.

The Cow, 1910
Oils on canvas, 95.5 × 105 cm

This picture is remarkable in several respects, for the spirit of synthesis that informs it, for its poetic treatment of a banal subject, and for the illustration it provides of ideas expounded in *Concerning the Spiritual in Art*.

In fact the work has all the qualities of a masterpiece, one of many produced by Kandinsky over a long and dedicated career. Although there is a narrative element (a milkmaid milking a cow), it is stated in equivocal terms, so that it is obvious this is not intended to be a 'genre' scene of the type favoured by painters in the realist tradition. A spatial hierarchy is respected, but the effect is of a primitivist work or a painting by a child (distant objects are very small, or elements are set out one on top of the other, as in the perspective of an oriental or medieval painting). The linear organization of the picture is deliberately ambiguous: the village appears to be perched on the end of the cow's back; the curve of the mountains and the town walls echo and reinforce the animal's undulating silhouette, and the cow's horn appears to coincide with a geological fault-line on the hillside . . . In the process of painting, reality is pulled and twisted out of shape, it is made fluid, so that the landscape and the scene depicted appear enigmatic, metamorphosed into that world of fairytale or fable that was one of Kandinsky's favourite themes.

Untitled (First Abstract Watercolour), *1910*
Pencil, watercolour and Indian ink, 49.6 × 64.8cm
(inscription on back: Watercolour 1910 [Abstract])

This famous watercolour, supposedly the world's first abstract painting, has been the subject of much controversy and debate.

There are two main schools of thought: according to the first, 1910 is the correct dating, and the picture belongs with a series of studies for *Composition VII*; the opposing view holds that the dating should be later, a stylistic comparison suggesting 1913. Evidence for this is the large format, unusual for the earlier date, and the more telling point that the work was entered late in the handwritten register of paintings kept by Kandinsky from 1919 onwards.

Whatever the truth of these conjectures, the watercolour itself is a particularly spontaneous piece of work, its light patches of colour enhanced by vigorous strokes of the pen in a 'sparklingly lively and fresh dance'. Execution apart, it demonstrates Kandinsky's bold pursuit of his objective of 'emancipating form'. Nevertheless, the picture's exaggerated fame should not blind us to the fact that it is essentially a sketch, no more than an exercise, whatever its importance in the development of painting.

KANDINSKY 1910

Lyrically, 1911
Oils on canvas, 94 × 130cm

'The artist who creates in full consciousness cannot be content with the object just as he represents it. He inevitably seeks to give it an expression. This is what used to be called idealization. Subsequently it has been known as stylization. Tomorrow there will no doubt be some other word for it.' So Kandinsky defines the progress of the artist away from 'the narrative appearance of the object . . . towards composition'.

On the other hand, in a footnote he specifies that 'stylization [in Impressionism] was not directed towards the embellishment of organic form . . . It conveyed a sound appropriate to it, but there was always an external element introduced that became dominant. In the future, the treatment to which the organic form will be submitted, and the transformations it will undergo, will be directed towards releasing that inner sound . . .' (*Concerning the Spiritual in Art*).

That is an apt description of Kandinsky's intentions in this picture; the linear design of springing curves draws the whole surface of the canvas together, transcribing the figure up to the point where it is cut off, as the horse's muzzle meets the frame. Movement and dynamism are expressed through the energetic calligraphy, which is punctuated by a few patches of colour enlivening the 'ground' of the picture. The strange title, with its reference to music and poetry, is unique of its kind, emphasizing the sonorous power of line liberated in a surge of pure energy.

Romantic Landscape, 1911
Oils on canvas, 94.3 × 129cm

This has almost the air of a manifesto picture. The 'blue riders' are unleashed in a headlong gallop over a landscape that is a blend of sky-blues and purples. Once again Kandinsky seems to be playing with words. If his landscape is 'romantic' it is not because of its wild magnificence or melancholy aspect, but rather because it conjures up the atmosphere of a spiritual quest, which the ride through perilously uncertain country is intended to evoke. The function of these horsemen is to awaken the vibration of un-suspected harmonies within a fragmented natural world, rather than merely to suggest the vanity of their efforts in pitting themselves against it.

Impression IV (Gendarme), 1911
Oils on canvas, 95 × 107cm

Of the 6 *Impressions*, all painted in 1911, this is the most famous. As Kandinsky himself pointed out, external nature is still distinguishable, albeit in an attenuated form. All that survives of the gendarme is his tricorn hat and a patch of colour suggesting his uniform. His mount looks more like a wooden rocking-horse than a fiery steed; its thick outline is no more than a pretext, a powerful element in the play of diagonals on which the composition is based.

The overall scheme of the painting is of quite breathtaking simplicity – yet it is still essentially traditional, since the illusion of depth is created by lines leading to a notional vanishing point. The innovations lie elsewhere. As in *The Cow*, reality is subtly pulled out of shape and distorted, and even the few narrative elements (a street, a fair and the vigilant presence of the mounted constable) leave much to the imagination – as is not inappropriate for an interpretation that has its share of irony and humour.

Composition IV, 1911
Oils on canvas, 159.5 × 250.5cm

There are 10 *Compositions* by Kandinsky, of which 7 were painted between 1910 and 1914.

By comparison with the *Impressions* and *Improvisations*, these are much more finished pieces, 'worked at over a long period . . . in an almost pedantic fashion', to use the painter's own words. In 1913, Kandinsky wrote an article explaining the complex gestation of his *Composition VI* (1913, Hermitage Museum, Leningrad), pointing out that he re-used elements from the earlier *Composition IV*: 'The fact that the whole consisted of a number of smaller forms created a need for something that would work in a very simple and broad [largo] way. For that purpose I employed long, imposing lines . . . These related to the heavy lines at the top which in turn led back to the precisely drawn diagonals, abutting directly onto them . . . To soften the over-dramatic resonance of the lines [an effect present, in his opinion, even in *Composition IV*], I allowed a veritable fugue of various shades of pink spots to play over the canvas [*Composition VI*].'

One sees here how the graphic elements acquire a different resonance, depending on the colours with which they are in tension. These is a preponderance of yellow and orange, which serve to temper the sharp, rather menacing, strong and precise lines of an ensemble that is, on the whole, tranquil in mood; green 'lends a touch of liveliness to the hot atmosphere and blues break up its character of calm solemnity', by producing an 'effect of inner warmth'.

Kandinsky describes his *Compositions* as 'symphonies', emphasizing their qualities of synthesis and polyphony, such that all the parts combine to give maximum cohesion to the finished work.

Oars, 1910
Watercolour and Indian ink on wove paper, 25 × 32cm

Improvisation 26 (Rowing), 1912
Oils on canvas, 97 × 107.5cm

A comparison of one of Kandinsky's most famous paintings with its preparatory study offers a revealing insight into the artist's working methods. Two years separate the two works. The graphic conciseness of the first is replaced in the second by a dominant chromatic dissolution. The stylized transcription of elements of reality in the sketch re-emerges in the painting daringly liberated from all figurative logic: blue and yellow (again the opposition Kandinsky loved) fill the centre of the canvas, but now there is no discernible reference to a figurative reality (the blue of the lake or the shadow of the mountain); the trees and figures are transformed into ideograms, of no obvious significance; the 'oars' survive only as dominant lines which urge us forward into the heart of the picture. The sole vestige of reality that remains is the line of the parapet, which Kandinsky retained not only here but in the various other studies he executed before embarking on the final canvas. Water, boats, lakes and mountains were favourite subjects for Kandinsky during his years in Murnau.

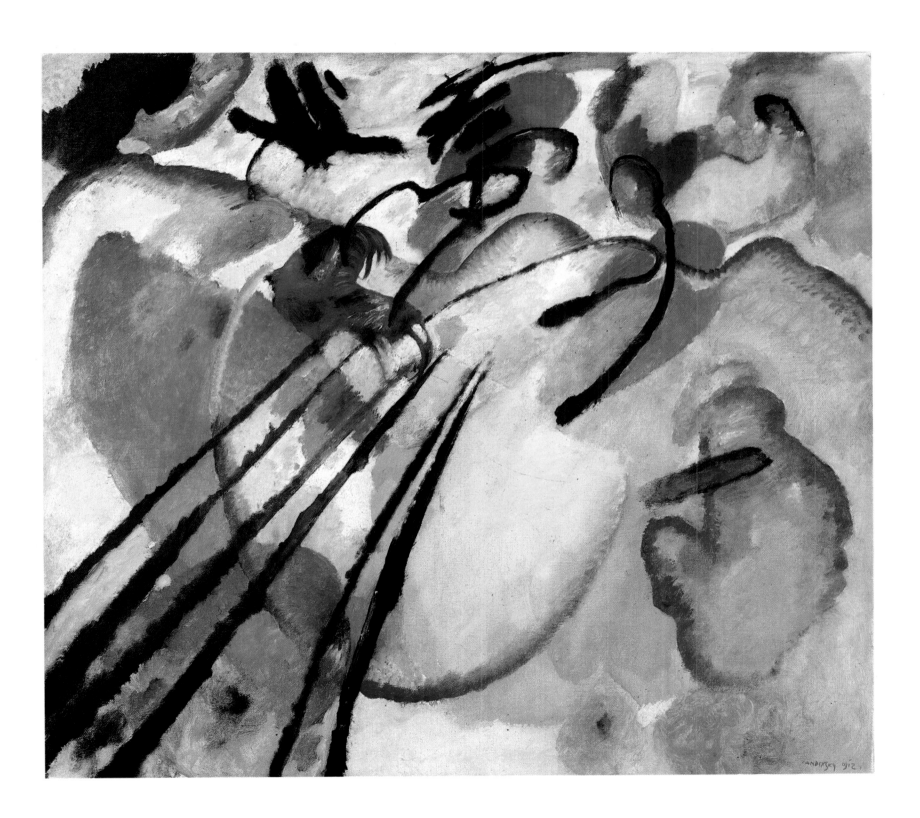

Painting with a Black Arch, 1912
Oils on canvas, 189 × 198cm

A work of major significance, this painting marks the culmination of the 'period of genius' spoken of by Grohmann.

The title *Painting with a Black Arch* derives from the painting's dominant feature; in that respect it is typical of the kind of title on which Kandinsky was to rely in the future to describe what he called 'absolute painting'.

On Kandinsky's insistence, the picture was exhibited in place of *Improvisation 27* at the Der Sturm gallery in Berlin. A critic interested in the painter's development noticed (not before time) that 'in this instance the object has been abandoned, so that one can think only in terms of the music of the forms . . .' Certainly Kandinsky himself was convinced that in *Painting with a Black Arch* he held the key to the future direction of his art. In August 1912, he wrote to Schoenberg: 'Up to now, construction has been understood to mean an insistent geometry (Holder, the Cubists etc.). But what I want to show is that construction can also be achieved – and better – by means of "the principle of dissonance", that it indeed offers far more potential, and that it is absolutely vital to demonstrate that potential as we leave the present age behind . . .'

In the prevailing creative climate, as Schoenberg himself was abandoning melodic line to write his first atonal composition, *Painting with a Black Arch* constituted a devastating attack on the expressionistic lyricism of the Post-Romantic sensibility. With the harmonies of its colours vibrating under the impact of the major chord of the black lines, it was a violent statement of opposition, and indeed had almost the character of an act of aggression.

Described as 'primitive giganticism' (K. Riethel), likened to 'three continents in collision' (W. Grohmann), *Painting with a Black Arch* attracted universal attention. It came to be regarded by the critics as the first true abstract painting, consisting uniquely of 'forms and colours' that were disposed by no other logic than that of the work's 'inner' model.

One is bound to say that the original Russian title is done less than justice in its French, German and English translations: initially there was not an 'arch' but a 'yoke', a reference to the roughly semi-circular shape of the harness that has been used by peasants since time immemorial. The Russian title suggests 'binding together', one of the functions Kandinsky intended his expressively drawn thick black line to fulfil, uniting the three masses of colour as well as holding them in tension.

The Last Judgement, 1912
Watercolour and Indian ink, painted on glass, 33.6 × 45.3cm

This is a typical glass-painting by Kandinsky, expressive of all the exuberance and spontaneity he experienced when using the process; he declared 'he knew almost no other kind of work that was so diverting'.

The technique of glass-painting had maintained its popularity in Germany. One of the factories that produced such items was in Murnau, and still in operation when Kandinsky lived there with Gabriele Münter. Sometimes Kandinsky and his friends, Marc and Macke, organized communal sessions devoted to the activity. Kandinsky held his pictures of this type in high esteem and they featured regularly in exhibitions of his work.

Study for 'Small Pleasures', 1913
Watercolour and Indian ink on laid paper, 23.8 × 31.5cm

The evocative title of this study (the final canvas is in the Guggenheim Museum, New York) almost speaks for itself. The space is filled with 'atomized' elements, among which can be seen the familiar motifs of the boat and the mountain, together with buildings that are typically Muscovite in appearance; at the same time there are a whole number of cancelling strokes, broken lines and embryonic spirals, which serve to create a confusion within the image. A sense of lightheartedness characterizes this chaotic accumulation of elements, as though Kandinsky was not over-concerned to find a dominant theme but was content to sit back and enjoy the luxuriance of the symphonic process.

Painting with Red Spot, 1914
Oils on canvas, 130 × 130cm

In 1914 Kandinsky produced few paintings, even though he was then at the peak of his abilities. He was preoccupied, in the grip of an obsession, something that was quite separate from his agonized reactions to the terrible destruction of the World War. Intolerant of any demands made on him, he wanted only to be left in peace and quiet.

Painting with Red Spot is one of the major works of that year, and reflects a new concern in Kandinsky's work. Here he is no longer preoccupied solely with liberating painting from the objective world, or with the telling combination of forms and colours in an apparent disorder. Divisionism of touch again characterizes the handling, but not now for the purpose of 'anti-naturalism', rather as a means of achieving shimmer and iridescence comparable to that of his glass-paintings. A process is used of covering a thin coat of pigment with a thicker binding medium, often of a whitish hue, and it is this that gives the picture its exceptional luminosity and surface animation.

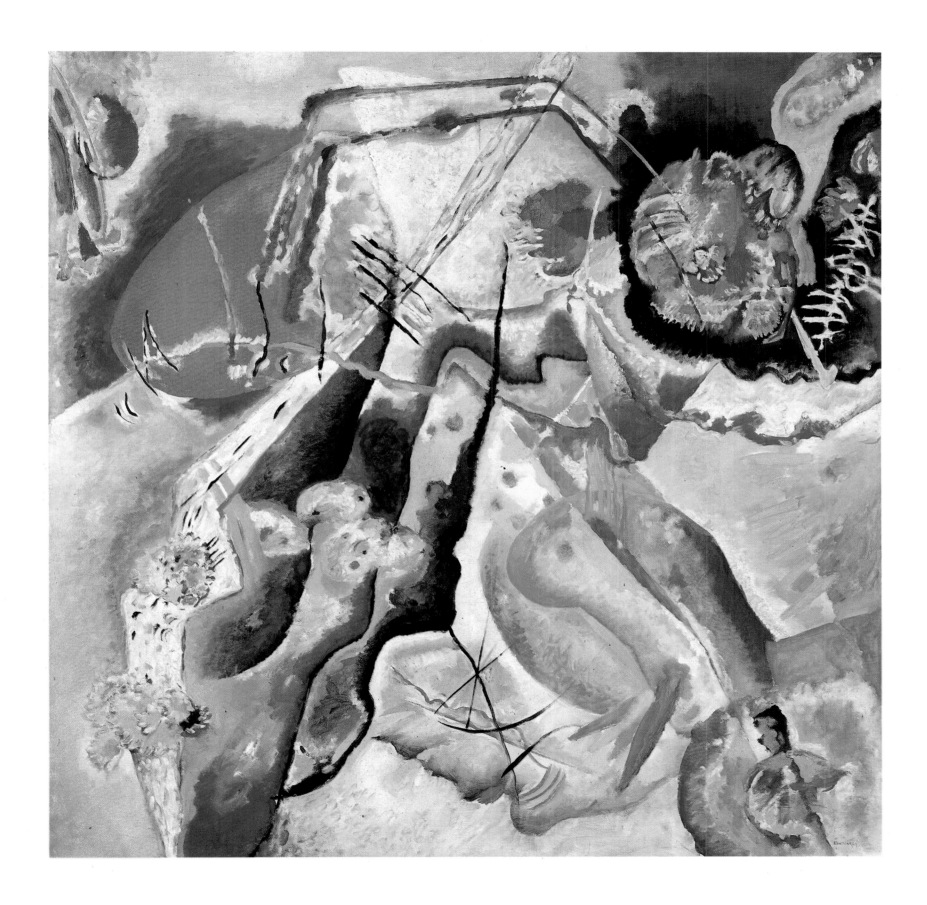

Painting on Light Ground, 1916
Oils on canvas, 100 × 78cm

In 1915, the year Kandinsky returned to Moscow, he painted no picture at all. Early in 1916, he was in Stockholm making preparations for an exhibition, and it was there that he executed *Painting on Light Ground*, the only oil-painting that has survived of the few produced in that year.

The image is set within an irregularly shaped 'frame' that barely extends to the edges of the canvas. Possibly Kandinsky was bored with the restrictions of orthodox formats, or, conceivably, he wanted to use the effect of distortion to introduce a feeling of movement.

The procedure seems unnecessarily laborious, and the matt colours and restrained palette are unappealing in comparison with some of Kandinsky's other works, in which he displays both his compositional abilities and his marvellous gifts as a colourist.

Untitled (Achtyrka), 1917
Oils on canvas, 27.5 × 33.6cm

1917 was the year of the October Revolution, in which Kandinsky took no direct part.

A year later he was nevertheless appointed to teach at the Vkhutemas (Moscow Studios of Free Art), and two years after that was made director of the Museum of Pictorial Culture.

It was a time of economic hardship for everyone, and survival was the highest priority.

Kandinsky made a conscious decision to return to figurative painting. This was partly to insure that he could make a living as an artist, and, with that in mind, he produced a number of works in the Biedermeier style then popular among the bourgeoisie of St Petersburg: insipid images of elegant women in crinolines and dandyish men in frock-coats. But above all he was overcome by a purely emotional reaction to being once again in Moscow, and he seized the chance to paint views of the city he loved, its cupolas reflecting the sunset in what he once described as a veritable symphony of colour; he also delighted in painting portraits of his wife Nina and scenes, like this one, set in or around the dacha where they stayed in the village of Achtyrka.

This figurative interlude is not to be interpreted as a renunciation of abstraction, merely as a reaction to a particular moment in Kandinsky's life, when a return to realism provided security and reassurance in the face of 'external' problems.

In Grey, 1919
Oils on canvas, 129 × 176cm

This large canvas could well have been included in the series of *Compositions*; it is highly complex, both in terms of its construction and the richness of its execution. Grohmann, however, finds it '. . . involved in the extreme and disturbing in its exuberance, produced no doubt in a spirit of experiment.'

One of the principal reasons for the painting's fame is that it is the only major work surviving from the years 1919 and 1920. Yet it is not fundamentally different from what preceded it, and in no sense to be regarded as a work of transition. On the contrary, the painting is fully achieved, combining 'abstract landscapes, elongated forms floating over a very complex background, in space, in an atmosphere characterized by insubstantial shades of grey'. The 'black arch' in the top left-hand corner of the picture – clearly an echo of *Painting with a Black Arch* of 1912 – tends rather to disappear among the superimposed rectangular planes on which it rests. Kandinsky himself said the work was: '. . . the conclusion of my dramatic period, the time when I built up such accumulations of forms.' The multiplicity of elements and subtly biomorphic figures were soon to give way to strict geometric forms, coinciding with Kandinsky's return to Germany and a period of intense concentration on oil painting from 1922 onwards.

Study for 'The Green Border', 1920
Watercolour and Indian ink, 26.9 × 36.3cm

Only the study of this motif has survived, the resultant oil painting having been lost some time after Kandinsky left Moscow.

The canvas is however referred to in Grohmann's biography: he notes that, in 1919, Kandinsky returned to work, painting 'a few watercolours and six oils: *Red Border, White Oval, The Green Border, Two Ovals . . .*' The list of titles gives an idea of Kandinsky's interests in and around 1920. Of particular note is the systematic exploitation of the irregular border already used in *Painting on Light Ground*. This 'figure outside the figure' serves to reinforce the containment of the dispersed forms, and it tends increasingly to become the dominant feature of the composition, as in the paintings of *Ovals*, where the effect is not so much of a frame containing a background as of a quasi-geometric form painted on to the canvas.

The use of circular or oval-shaped canvases is rare in Kandinsky's work. The expression of inner necessity was largely incompatible with a form that was already an 'object' in its own right, although on occasion, as in this study, particularly felicitous results could be obtained by abandoning the traditional neutrality of the white page.

Black Spot, 1921
Oils on canvas, 137 × 120cm

'The combination of curved with broken lines, each with its own characteristics, achieves an amplified sonority,' wrote Kandinsky in the second chapter of *Point and Line to Plane*.

Here we see just such grids of intersecting lines, caught in an upward movement. Chromatic punctuations are provided by the three almost perfect circles in primary colours, which occupy the lower register of the picture, and are triumphantly united in the dominant black spot, fringed with brown, on which our attention is focused by the complex patterns of lines converging upon it. The picture is a strikingly apt illustration of Kandinsky's theoretical ideas. It is impressive too for its absolute clarity and extreme economy of means, characteristic of Kandinsky's new style, in which calculation takes precedence over spontaneity, and geometric precision over organic disorder.

Black Grid, 1922
Oils on canvas, 96 × 106cm

At this period of his life, Kandinsky was teaching at the Bauhaus, in Weimar. The atmosphere was stimulating and his work resumed a regular pattern, progressing smoothly.

There were two particularly significant developments in Kandinsky's painting during those Bauhaus years: first – and this canvas is a particularly fine example – he began to combine elements derived from his Russian and Munich-based works with geometric forms; and second, he opted definitely for the use of pure geometric shapes, according to the principles developed in *Point and Line to Plane*.

The other interesting feature of this picture is its espousal of certain features of Malevich's Suprematism, so that it is effectively Kandinsky's response to the aesthetic views propounded by that other great master of abstract art. For Malevich, forms acquired an autonomy that enabled them to float in the space of the canvas, or even move across it; space was an artifice to be exploited by the artist. *Black Square* and *White Square on a White Background* were the paintings that marked this radical departure in Malevich's work, from 1915/16 onwards.

In *Yellow Square*, for example, the square, set at an angle, becomes a trapezium, and seems to bury itself in the surface of the canvas, or emerge out of it. It becomes a second two-dimensional plane, which literally 'crosses' the square plane of the canvas. In later paintings, this leads on to a proliferation of flat-painted rectangles, splitting apart or superimposed, apparently freed from the control of the canvas on which they are drawn, content merely to brush against it, penetrate it, occasionally even come to rest upon it, in a perpetual ballet of polygons and trapeziums that corresponds to Malevich's declared intention of creating a fourth dimension, representing time.

If Kandinsky seems here to take over Malevich's theories in a wholesale fashion, he does also introduce concepts that are purely his own. Triangles, rectangles, circles and square float in space, but it is 'inhabited' space, created out of the 'inner necessity' that was central to his view of creativity. The space in question is no longer the off-white of the canvas but a *painted* space, occupied by figures and filled with pleasing sensations and vibrations of colour. As for the 'black square', it has transformed itself into a polygonal grid which, with the benefit of Kandinsky's analysis of line, we know represented for him peace and tranquillity. *Black Grid* has a mood of gentle relaxation, the elements seem to glide smoothly through it rather than merely 'float'. And that atmosphere is strengthened by the seemingly paradoxical inclusion of two boats and two fishes, in the left-hand corner, moving unconcernedly through a calm sea.

Maquette of panel for the Juryfreie Exhibition, 1922
Gouache on black paper, 34.7 × 60cm

The project for a large mural, designed originally to be placed in the octagonal entrance hall of the Museum of New Art in Berlin, did not come to fruition in Kandinsky's lifetime. It was finally 'reproduced' on its intended scale in 1977, at the Pompidou Centre in Paris. There it forms part of the decoration of an entrance hall to the permanent collections of the Musée d'Art Moderne.

Kandinsky's original designs were produced in association with pupils following the course in mural painting at the Bauhaus. The paintings were subsequently exhibited at the Juryfreie Kunstschau, where they received a mixed reception from the critics. Although Katherine S. Dreier (who, in 1923, was to put on an exhibition of Kandinsky's work under the auspices of the Société Anonyme, in New York) was enthusiastic, the art critic of the review *Das Kunstblatt* expressed his disapproval in a single devastating comment: '. . . the result, a *chinoiserie*, in which the artist, always a talented decorator, seems at last to have found himself.' That assessment, its spiteful intention apart, does raise the whole question of the importance of the decorative element in Kandinsky's painting, a problem which has bothered some critics. Kandinsky himself was well aware there was a paradox, and it was a subject very much at the centre of his concerns during the period the Bauhaus was based in Weimar.

Through-going Line, 1923
Oils on canvas, 141 × 202cm

The long diagonal that sweeps across the canvas serves as the pivot on which the picture depends; the work as a whole is a highly typical illustration of Kandinsky's approach to forms during this period. There is a certain symmetry in the composition, with circle corresponding to circle, and the bluish-coloured trapezium echoing the trapezium-grid in the upper section. The large triangle, coloured yellow – ultimate emblem of spirituality in Kandinsky's pantheon of colours – lends the whole composition an upward movement. In fact, in this canvas, everything is in motion, solely because of the powerful device of the diagonal axis that slices across it, countering the apparent tendency of the geometric forms to fly off in the opposite direction.

The sobriety of the palette reinforces the tension of the linear effects, reflecting Kandinsky's intense interest, during 1923, in the potential of line, in the terms he set out in *Point and Line to Plane*.

In the Black Circle, 1923
Oils on canvas, 130 × 130cm

Kandinsky regarded the circle as the ideal figure, that which was both the simplest and the most formally assertive.

Complete in itself, a single contained inner tension, the circle possessed too a gravitational field, capable of attracting or repelling straight or curving lines within its ambit. It also had the ability to take on different aspects within the picture, its expressive plentitude transformed, depending on its position, into a star, a dot or an atom. Here the circle swells in size to become the picture itself, image identified with image, figure with figure. The effect would not have been the same if Kandinsky had simply used a circular canvas, for here the black circle is inscribed within a square, without actually touching its sides; the narrow border of space that is left, and the slightly irregular, hazy outline of the figure, make the circle appear to rise up out of the background on which it is drawn, emphasizing the sensation of implosion.

On White II, 1923
Oils on canvas, 105 × 98cm

This canvas, which bears the same title as one painted in Moscow in 1920, retains certain formal characteristics of Malevich's Suprematism – and indeed has certain affinities with that aesthetic system. Even so, these influences are transposed within a complex tension of diagonal lines that is entirely Kandinsky's.

The motif of intersecting diagonals recurs in a number of works painted during 1923, but this is the most developed statement of the theme. The precise matt-coloured triangles and trapeziums suspended over a white ground are strongly reminiscent of Suprematism, yet Kandinsky's approach to the combination of forms, the grammar of their composition, gives the painting an entirely different impact: here, the geometrical elements appear to be exploding outwards in a movement of centrifugal force.

Contact, 1924
Oils on canvas, 79 × 54cm

The central figure of this picture, the triangle, was – together with the circle – one of Kandinsky's favourite figures. He regarded it as a precise metaphor of spiritual enlightenment, a 'pyramid of humanity', its apex occupied by the small number of elect.

Here the form is inverted, and acts as the link between two circles, barely touching the lower one with its sharp point, and merging into the other at one of its upper angles. Bearing in mind the spiritual symbolism with which Kandinsky's forms are invested, one may legitimately read into this a parable of genesis – the transformation effected by contact with the life-giving triangle. That figure is perfectly balanced on its tip, as though demonstrating its spiritual equilibrium. A row of smaller triangles hover in the bottom left-hand corner, like an echo or confirmation of the major theme, one to which Kandinsky returned in *On Points*, developing his ideas further.

Upward Tension, 1924
Pencil, Indian ink, brown ink and watercolour, 48.7 × 33.7cm

Kandinsky's titles are by now beautifully apt descriptions of the works to which they are applied; frequently, as here, they suggest the process that is illustrated or examined in the picture.

There are a number of works with 'tension' in the title (*Red Tension*, *Hard Tension*, etc.), in many of which the colour red predominates.

For Kandinsky, 'the absolute sonority of forms depends on three factors, varying according to (1) the sonority of the straight lines in their variations, (2) the sonority of the inclination in relation to tensions of more or less force, (3) the sonority of a tendency towards a dominance, more or less total, of the plane.'

The fan of diagonals that extends out from the bottom left-hand corner of this picture has the effect of creating an upward movement, which 'tenses' the whole pictorial space and forces it towards the top. That rising sensation is however countered by a succession of crosses, which lead us towards a notional nucleus at the picture's heart.

Contrasting Sounds, 1924
Oils on canvas, 70 × 49.5 cm

The sensual emphasis of this painting is unusual among the works of the earlier Bauhaus period, which Kandinsky himself described as characteristically 'cold'.

The precise reasons for this difference are to be sought in the untypical handling, the liberal use of impasto, the subdivision even of geometric figures into a number of smaller parts, and the prevalence of hazy aureoles drawn concentrically around the circles.

The picture is perhaps best regarded as illustrating a precise area of Kandinsky's experimentation, one strand in the programme of research he pursued so energetically in the favourable surroundings of the Bauhaus. The title gives a clue to his intentions: to bring contrasting geometrical elements into a complementary accord, and to make that accord survive even while subject to divergent tensions. Kandinsky's investigations of a 'breaking point', and his combinations of dissimilar elements (here the circle and the square), were to form the basis of later pictures built around the symmetrical repetition of similar forms.

Yellow-Red-Blue, 1925
Oils on canvas, 128 × 201.5cm

The title here carries an echo of the theories of Neo-Plasticism, according to which painting had to be restricted to the primary colours and the three non-colours (black, grey and white) as a means of combating the tendency towards Naturalism.

While Kandinsky was no lover of 'objective nature', quite the reverse in fact, he did not share the asceticism and doctrinal rigidity of painters like Mondrian or van Doesburg.

In this picture Kandinsky respects the spiritual correspondences of forms and colours, using yellow for the triangle, red for the square and blue for the circle. Furthermore, the system is extended to cover the areas of influence of those forms, so that on the left-hand side of the canvas, in the area marked by two oblique lines, the dominant colour is a strident yellow; the right-hand side is stamped with a heavy undulating line; and, finally, the centre is occupied by a number of indistinct dark-red parallelepipeds.

Some have chosen to see in this canvas the expression of a conflict or opposition, symbolized by the different 'weights' of the colours yellow and blue. If there is a conflict, then it exists at a purely theoretical level, and relates to the relative importance accorded to the circle and the triangle in Kandinsky's work at this time.

Accent in Pink, 1926
Oils on canvas, 100.5 × 80.5 cm

This painting has to be looked at in conjunction with *Some Circles*, executed in the same year. In that picture, a number of coloured circles are set against a neutral black ground; these appear to palpitate and multiply, in an incandescence of coloured auras emanating from a patch of unbroken blue, spreading out from a central nucleus like a constellation of stars or a planetary system in the process of being formed.

It is the same motif that occupies the central section of this painting, so that what we have here is a 'picture-within-a-picture'. Using the clue provided by the title – now always descriptive of the work's intent – it is not difficult to understand Kandinsky's purposes in his restatement of the theme. In this new configuration of spawning circles (an image of expansion), there is one figure that is dominant. A large circular splash of Tyrian pink, it is both the culmination of the process (because it has reached the greatest size) and also the most threatening of the elements present, boring at the canvas, apparently eating right into it, destroying the very thing that brought it into existence.

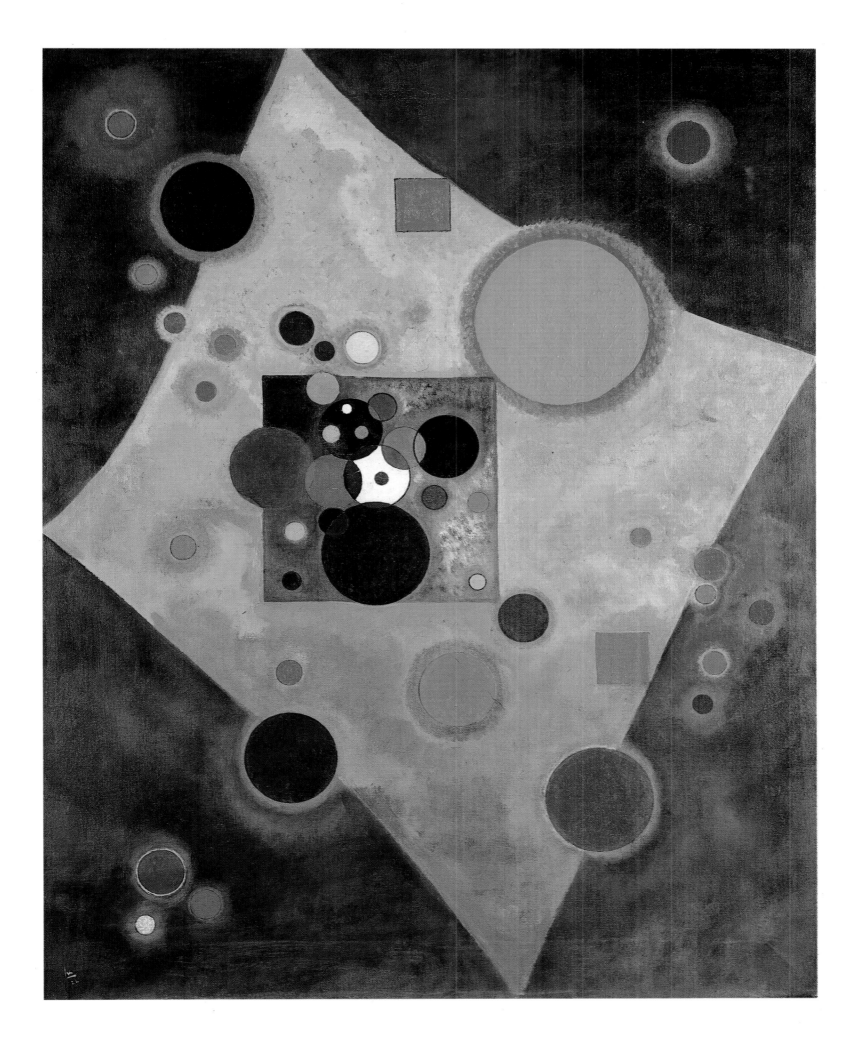

Soft Hard, 1927
Oils on canvas, 33 × 41.5 cm.

All the resources of line are exploited here in an orchestration of the basic forms, circle, triangle and square. Yet the stark simplicity of the formal arrangement is tempered by the subtle colouring of the figures. It is as though Kandinsky is seeking to make a deliberate statement, to the effect that formal purity can no longer exist once colour is introduced. Indeed one is almost tempted to believe that the picture is directed specifically against the rigours of Constructivism, that its flat colours actually work in opposition to the forms, creating a skin over them, and denying their absolute validity. In fact, of course, it is overwhelmingly the process of 'inner necessity' that dictates this outcome; the sensuality of expression is a necessary accompaniment to the drive towards the spiritualization of forms, in which at the same time they become 'humanized'. Abstraction may be 'immaterial', but it must also be made flesh, for it cannot exist beyond the reach of the real world, or at least that part of reality which the artist himself encompasses. Thus it is possible to see here a kind of parable of creativity, in which the concentric circles appear as the pupil of an eye, and the triangle represents inert muscular tissue; at the same time, the infinite empty spaces of sky-blue may be said to symbolize creation in its topographical and cosmogenic aspects. Kandinsky is not unaware that the Word was made flesh, but his logic also tells him that only a transmutation brought about through feeling is capable of reconciling the human with the divine, or discipline with freedom; it alone is rooted in spiritual harmony that makes no distinction between divine nature and nature as a speculative on-going force.

On Points, 1928
Oils on canvas, 140 × 140cm

This shifting geometry of figures inscribed within a perfect square illustrates Kandinsky's concept of the surface plane, following on from his theories of point and line. Indeed the title of his book *Point and Line to Plane* accurately reflects his methodology, of relating the operations of the two former elements to the exigencies of the latter. Kandinsky establishes a precise relationship between the moment in which form is generated (the point, or dot), its development and emergence into identity (space contained by line) and its situation (the space, or plane, within which the form is contained).

Kandinsky regarded the square as the most objective form of the 'original' or surface plane, since '. . . its boundaries possess the same tonal intensity. Hot and cold are held in balance'. The artist's task is to '. . . impregnate . . . this being with the right elements in the right places'. The way the forms are distributed, in relation to the boundaries of the virgin surface plane, sets up different intensities and resistances. In this canvas, the whole composition is shifted to the right (starting with the base of three parallel lines), with the sole exception of the large circle supported by its triangular armature, which tends to push upwards and move towards the top left-hand corner.

Although the title makes explicit reference to the ballerina's technique of dancing 'on points', perfectly balanced, the configuration of the whole, and the discreet palette, serve to unite circles and triangles in the metaphorical figure of a gigantic hot-air balloon, a motif used by Kandinsky on many subsequent occasions.

Light, 1930
Oils on board, 69 × 48cm

In the appendix to *Point and Line to Plane*, plate 15 shows an example of the 'relationship of a curved line to the point'. Although *Point and Line to Plane* is not to be regarded as a dictionary of forms, or a source-book for Kandinsky's motifs, there are evident similarities between that illustration and this picture. The picture is, however, more complex, and the introduction of a number of elements of 'disturbance' serves both to make the design less schematic and to make it clear that, once again, it is the 'relationship to the original plane' with which Kandinsky is particularly concerned – in this instance, the creation of a graphic sequence that perfectly 'matches' its coloured support, causing it to be no longer static but mobile. Thus, the swelling form of the curve is accompanied by a swirling haze, following its upward path, and a short horizontal line is placed in the top right-hand corner, blocking the ripple of concentric waves. This discreet echo of the picture edge performs an important function; apparently a 'light' interjection, it actually provides a fixed point in the image, and, by preventing it from going 'out of frame', safeguards the integrity of the 'surface plane'.

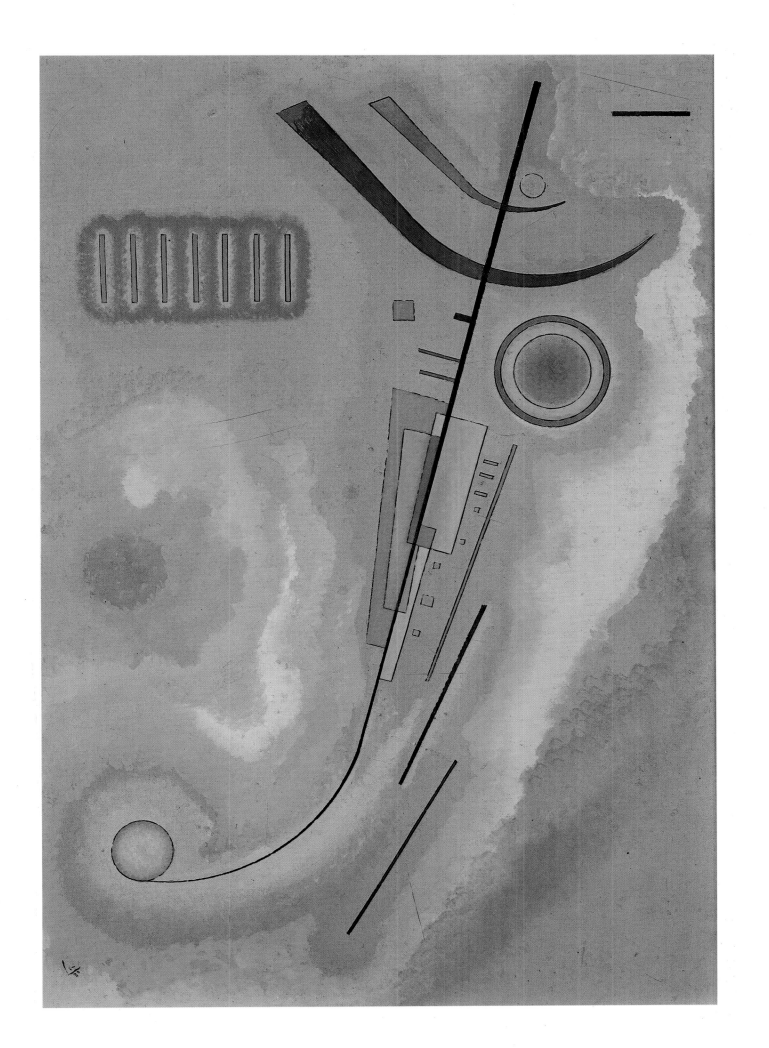

Thirteen Rectangles, 1930
Oils on board, 69.5 × 59.5 cm

Radically restricting the means of expression, reducing his formal vocabulary to its essentials, Kandinsky produces here an exercise in asceticism. In the course of 1930 he executed a number of canvases in a similar spirit (*Two Squares, Trapezium, Striped*), confirmation of his belief that a 'single colour or form may be made the basis of a composition'.

Although the central rectangle is painted red (the appropriate colour for that figure, according to Kandinsky's system), the rest are in subtle gradations of colour, and arranged with apparent illogicality; the effect is to disrupt the static quality of the whole and introduce a 'kinetic' element, foreshadowing the optical experiments in painting during the post-war years.

Two Green Points, 1935
Oil and sand on canvas, 114 × 162cm

There is an almost universal critical reaction that the title of this picture is inappropriate. At around this time Kandinsky used many rather similar titles, based on the notion of a pair of matching elements, but here the two 'green dots' could hardly be said to be the central feature of the composition.

Yet one notices them immediately: they are like two eyes looking straight into our own. Indeed, so strong is the anthropomorphism of the image that they are in danger of obliterating all the rest from our consciousness. Kandinsky was almost uncannily prescient when he wrote: 'A small form may be given such a strong "accent" that it entirely changes its size and intensity, and in the process, the importance of the rest.'

This picture is a perfect demonstration of what Kandinsky meant, and it is not fanciful to suppose that he took a certain calculated pleasure in choosing his title, designed to focus our attention on precisely the element that is most ambiguous in its function.

The White Line, 1936
Gouache, tempera on black paper, 49.9 × 38.7cm

In flight from Nazi Germany, Kandinsky moved in 1933 to Paris. His critical reputation was generally assured, he was respected by a number of front-rank artists, among them Miró, and he received offers of help and encouragement from André Breton and, above all, Jeanne Bucher, who showed his work in her gallery. Yet his financial situation was not secure. As well as major canvases (*Dominant Curve, Composition X*), he also produced a number of small gouaches intended for immediate sale; these he judged minor works.

This particular gouache is one for which Kandinsky had a certain affection and esteem.

The White Line is an example of the 'lyrical geometry' to which Kandinsky turned at this time. Although in many respects typical of the work of this period, notably for its biomorphic structure, it is unusual both in being painted on a black ground, that of the paper itself, and for its use of tempera.

Composition IX, 1936
Oils on canvas, 113.5 × 195 cm

We know that Kandinsky reserved the title *Composition* for exceptional large-scale works, 'developed slowly and worked at over a long period', in which 'intelligence, consciousness, and lucid intent play a capital role'. But, he added, 'it is not calculation that is the principal thing, it is intuition.' This *Composition IX* is the second-to-last work to bear that name, and some have questioned Kandinsky's choice of the title, preferring *Dominant Curve*, painted in the same year and, even in the artist's own opinion, a more fully achieved piece of work.

The canvas is of a rather confusing complexity. The division of the background into diagonal bands of colour is, for a start, unique in Kandinsky's *oeuvre*, and the 'transfer' motifs are suspended over their coloured fields in a rather precarious profusion. Overall, there is an irritating sense of incompleteness, even though it is an impression contradicted by the title.

Hedonistic in mood, the picture reflects Kandinsky's delight at his immersion, during this time, in the physical processes of painting.

Centre with Accompaniment, 1937
Oils on canvas, 114 × 146cm

A veritable phantasmagoria of forms, this picture shows why Breton and the Surrealists were so interested in Kandinsky. It is highly reminiscent of Miró and Magnelli and all that strand of painting that concerns itself with poetry and subconscious imagery, rather than with the eradication of meaning from the image. The extraordinary and fantastic figures with which Kandinsky filled his canvases at this time have been described variously as jelly-fish, amoebae and coral organisms, on the one hand, or echoes of Scythian symbols and Oriental jewellery on the other. The Parisian period at the end of Kandinsky's career is particularly difficult to come to terms with, and critical opinion remains strictly divided.

Although filled with a proliferation of 'creatures', these paintings are nevertheless a logical extension of Kandinsky's work at the Bauhaus. The profusion of signs cannot conceal the strength of that same underlying impulse, to express 'inner nature' by means of line and colour. Grohmann quite rightly warns against the temptation to see in these forms 'the least analogy with any specific finished form', reminding us that 'it is the construction that forces the association'.

Many-coloured Ensemble, 1938
Oils and mixed media on canvas, 116 × 89cm

The initial impression of this image is that it represents a cell, viewed under a microscope. Two considerations serve to dispel that illusion: first, Kandinsky's original French title of *Entassement réglé*, which suggests above all a *regulated* combination of formal elements; secondly, the polyphony of the colours, which have little or nothing to do with the natural world.

The fact that Kandinsky hesitated between the two titles would tend to indicate that he regarded both these aspects of the picture as significant, complementary to each other.

There is also a sense in which the painting is a re-examination of a problem with which Kandinsky had been much exercised in the past: that of the insertion of one form within another (see *In the Black Circle*). If the 'soft geometry' of the larger form is a corruption of the circle, then it is entirely logical that the elements it contains should be of a correspondingly organic complexity.

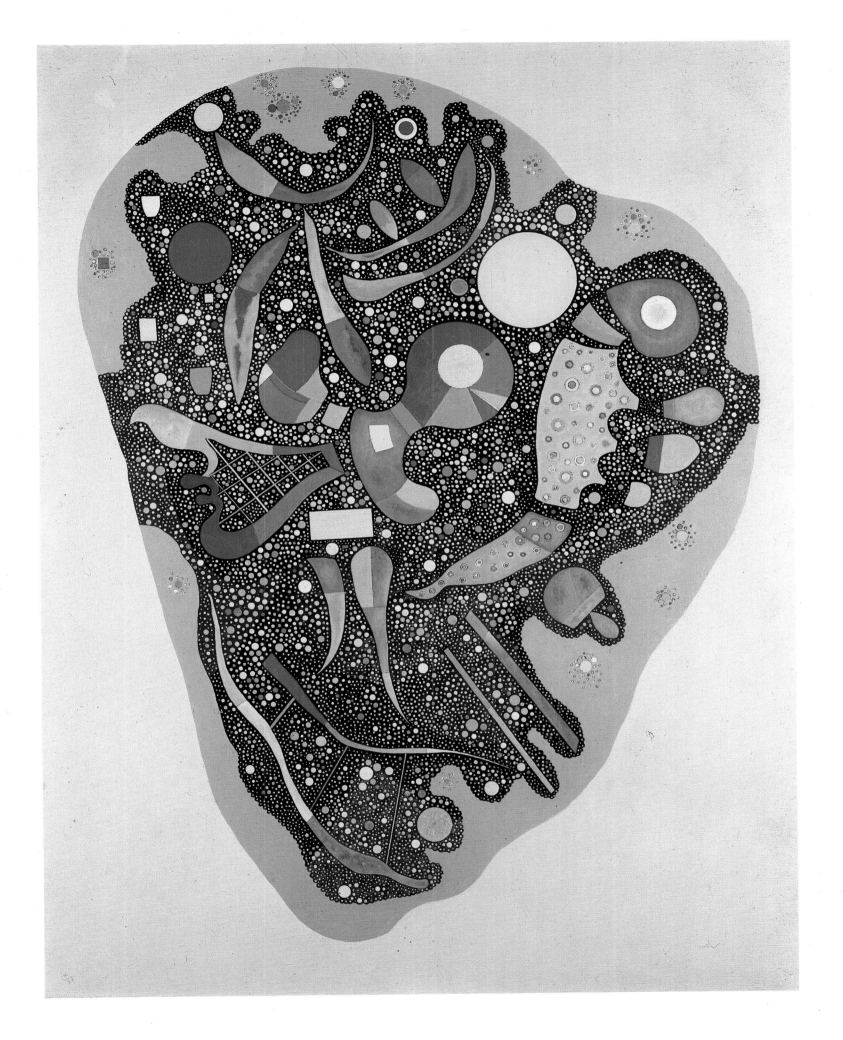

Composition X, 1939
Oils on canvas, 130 × 195 cm

The last of the great 'compositions', **this** canvas is unique in the series in having a black background, rarely used by Kandinsky except for certain of the gouaches. Yet the opaque ground is a particularly effective enhancement of the luxuriance and brilliance of the colours, and the profusion of the figures. The mood here is celebratory, and an atmosphere of heightened fantasy prevails. As in some of Kandinsky's pictures from his Murnau period (*The Cow, Impression IV* [*Gendarme*]), it is possible to detect a certain narrative content. A face with a querulous comma seems to look at an air-balloon attached to its gondola, while sheets of writing are blown in the wind. The large brown patch is filled with fine streaks and squiggles of colour, a sequence of hieroglyphs that hints at some magical significance or enchantment.

It is not surprising that such a display of light-hearted optimism was misunderstood in some quarters, at a time when the continent was about to be plunged into war.

Sky Blue, 1940
Oils on canvas, 100 × 43cm

Is this picture to be seen as yet another expression of carefree optimism, painted even as Paris was under occupation? Did Kandinsky simply blot out the reality, taking refuge in a world of dreams and fantasy?

The title alone would tend to confirm that view. Although Kandinsky had long since ceased to use titles descriptive of anything other than pictorial elements or processes, here the reference, with its overtones of escapism (especially in the original French), is too direct to be mistaken: the background here is not just an expanse of colour, it is the enticing clear blue of the sky itself. The creatures floating about in the atmosphere have been variously interpreted as fantastic micro-organisms, or hybrids of birds, fishes or turtles. Yet they are not the true subject of the picture. Their presence serves rather to reveal the unsullied calm and infinite sweep of this expanse of sky.

Reciprocal Accord, 1942
Oils and mixed media on canvas, 114 × 146cm

This is one of the last major paintings by Kandinsky. The title is ambiguous: is it simply a description of the symmetrical, balanced forms on the canvas, or does it contain a more personal reference, perhaps to the sense of satisfaction experienced by the artist in painting the picture?

A work of supreme assurance and maturity, in its elegant complexity it stands out among the exuberance and excess to which Kandinsky was on occasion tempted.

The clarity of the construction – two triangular masses revolving around a central axis formed by the white space in the centre of the canvas – and the subtly orchestrated interplay of line and colour, these all combine to make a living whole, striking just that 'perfect note' that was the painter's ultimate goal. Colour and form, sign and line, are inseparable one from the other.

When Vassily Kandinsky died in December 1944, his widow Nina placed the open coffin in his studio, with an easel on either side. The paintings she chose to display were *Movement I* and *Reciprocal Accord*.

Tempered Elan, 1944
Oils on board, 42 × 58cm

In the last two years of his life, Kandinsky produced a quantity of drawings and paintings in gouache and Indian ink. When he turned to oil-painting (which demanded a much more intense effort of concentration), it was always on boards of modest dimensions.

Tempered Elan stands as a fitting conclusion to this Paris period, which has given rise to such misunderstanding, tending either to be neglected or dismissed by biographers of the artist. Two more recent studies have redressed the balance somewhat, by relating the changed emphasis in Kandinsky's work to other contemporary developments in painting. In the Paris of the thirties a number of interesting experiments were being conducted with a form of 'object-painting', in which everyday items were shown suspended against an abstract background (Léger, for example, used bunches of keys and pairs of scissors). The depiction of objects suspended in space became practically a pictorial convention, tying in with a revival of Futurist 'aero-painting' – and also coinciding with Miró's commencement of his series of *Constellations*. There was too, at this time, a strong current of interest in 'concrete art' which, without being figurative, made use of stylized and recomposed elements of reality.

Kandinsky discussed his position at length in two articles on 'L'Art concret', published in the first issue of the *Revue du XXe siècle*, March 1938. He had felt the need to escape from the impasse of geometric abstract painting, as it was being perpetuated by the successors of Neo-Plasticism who founded the 'Circle and Square' group. It was in this spirit that he began to investigate the possibilities of 'biological metamorphosis', and so found himself returning to certain aspects of naturalism.

Kandinsky was not doctrinaire. It was a remorseless quest for new forms that urged him on. At the end of his life he had no hesitation in 'tempering' that creative 'élan' that had carried him to the very limits of geometrical abstraction.

SHORT BIBLIOGRAPHY

Written Works by Kandinsky

Concerning the Spiritual in Art
Concerning the Spiritual in Art, translated by M. T. Sadler, London, Dover, 1977.
The Blue Rider
Der Blaue Reiter, Munich, R. Piper & Co, 1912.
L'Almanach du Blaue Reiter, édité par Mme Brion-Guerry, Paris, Klinksieck, 1981.
Sounds
Sounds, translated by E. R. Napier, London, Yale, 1981.
A Review of the Past
Ruckblicke, in Kandinsky 1901-1913, Berlin, Der Sturm, 1913.
Regards sur le Passé and other texts, 1912-1922, presented by J-P. Bouillon, Paris, Hermann, 1974.
Point and Line to Plane
Punkt und Linie zu Fläche: Beitrag zur Analyse der Malerischen Elemente, Bauhaus-Buch No. 9, Munich, 1926.
Point, Ligne, Plan: contribution to the analysis of pictorial elements, translated by Suzanne and Jean Leppien, Paris, Denoël-Gonthier Bibliothèque Méditations, 1970.
Courses at the Bauhaus
Cours du Bauhaus, translated by Suzanne and Jean Leppien, Paris, Denoël-Gonthier, Bibliothèque Méditations, 1975.
Complete Written Works
Wassily Kandinsky, Ecrits Complets, edited by Philippe Sers, Paris, Denoël-Gonthier, Vols 2 and 3, 1970 and 1975.

Works on Kandinsky

FRINEBERG, Johnathan, *Kandinsky in Paris, 1906-7*. U.M.I. Research, P.U.S., 1984.
GROHMANN, Will, *Vassily Kandinsky, Life and Work*, Harry N. Abrams Inc., New York, 1958.
KANDINSKY, Nina, *Kandinsky et Moi*, Flammarion, Paris, 1978.
LACOSTE, Pierre, *Kandinsky*, Clematis, London, 1979.
ROETHEL, Hans Konrad and BENJAMIN, Jean K., *Kandinsky*, Hudson Hills, New York, 1984.
ROETHEL, Hans Konrad and BENJAMIN, Jean K., *Catalogue Raisonné of the Oil Paintings*, 2 vols. Sotheby's Publications, London, 1982 and 1984.
VOLBOUDT, Pierre, *Kandinsky*, translated by Jane Brenton, Art Data, 1986.

Principal Exhibition Catalogues

BOISELL, Jessica and DEROUET, Christian, *Kandinsky*, Collections from the MNAM, Centre Georges Pompidou, Paris, 1984.
DEROUET, Christian, *Kandinsky: trente peintures des Musées soviétiques*, MNAM, Centre Georges-Pompidou, Paris, 1979.
MESSER, Thomas, *Wassily Kandinsky, a retrospective exhibition, 1866-1944*, The Solomon R. Guggenheim Museum, New York, 1963. Collectives: *Kandinsky in Munich, 1896-1914*, 1982. *Kandinsky: Russian and Bauhaus Years, 1915-1933*, 1983. *Kandinsky, the Paris Years, 1933-1944*, The Solomon R. Guggenheim Museum, New York, 1985. *Kandinsky Album*: MNAM, Centre Georges Pompidou, Paris, 1984.

CHRONOLOGY

1866
Wassily Kandinsky is born in Moscow on the 4th of December. There is Mongolian descent on his father's side. His mother is a muscovite.
1869
Trip to Italy with his parents. His first memories of colour impressions: the white (in Russia) of the wood of a stick the bark of which has been removed, the black (in Italy) of a carriage and a gondola.
1871
The Kandinsky family settles in Odessa.
1874
Music lessons: piano, then cello.
1876
Enters secondary school. Learns German.
1880 (or around 1880)
Purchase of his first box of paints.
1886
Returns to Moscow in order to take up law studies. Specializes in political economy. Takes part in the student struggles.
1889
Study trip (on peasant law) in the northern province of Vologda, in the course of which he becomes interested in the local decorative art. Visits the World Fair in Paris.
1892
Sits law examinations.
Marries his cousin Anya Chimiakine. Second trip to Paris.
1893
Agrégation in law. Lecturer in the Moscow Faculty of Law.
1895
Discovers Monet during the exhibition of French Impressionists in Moscow and a performance of Lohengrin at the Bolshoi. Becomes artistic director for the Kouchverev printing house in Moscow.
1896
Refuses a chair at the University of Dorpat (Estonia) and leaves to study painting in Munich. He is 30 years old.
1897
Enrols in the school of Anton Azbé where he meets his compatriots Marianne Werefkin and Alexis Jawlensky. He remains there for 2 years.
1899
Studies only drawing.
1900
Enters the class of F. von Stuck at the Munich Academy. First pictures.
1901
Founding of the group 'Phalanx' over which he will preside the following year.
1902
Opens a school of painting separate from the 'Phalanx'. Exhibits at the Secession in Berlin. First woodcuts. Meets Gabriele Münter who will become his companion.
1903
Closure of his school and trips to Venice and Russia.

1904
Dissolution of the group 'Phalanx'. Fresh travels (Holland, Odessa, Tunisia.)
Exhibits in various European cities including Paris.
'Poetry without words', an album of twelve woodcuts, comes out in the Stroganov Editions in Moscow.

1905
Stays in Odessa, Dresden and Rapallo. He exhibits across Europe.

1906
Starting from June he spends a year in Sèvres, near Paris.
An album of woodcuts appears in Tendances Nouvelles editions.

1907
Summer in Switzerland then winter in Berlin.

1908
Returns to Munich where he will stay for another six years. His first stay in Murnau. On intimate terms with Jawlensky and Marianne Werefkin.

1909
Buys a house in Murnau. President of the Neue Kunstlervereinigung (NKV) which has just been founded. First 'Improvisations'.

1910
Meets Franz Marc. Second exhibition of the NKV. Travels in Russia. Compiles *The Spiritual in Art*. The 'First Abstract Watercolour' probably dates from this year.

1911
Divorce from Anya Chimiakine. Makes friends with Klee, Macke, Arp, Schönberg, corresponds with Delaunay. Resigns from the NKV following the rejection of his 'Composition V' and with Franz Marc founds the group the 'Blaue Reiter' (Blue Rider). Becomes interested in the theme of Saint George, from which the name of the group perhaps derives. First exhibition of the group at the end of the year, at the Tanhäuser gallery.

1912
Publication of *The Spiritual in Art*, and of the *Almanach du Blaue Reiter*. First large one-man exhibition at the gallery of *Der Sturm* in Berlin in October. Trip to Russia.

1913
An exhibition at Bock's in Hamburg is fiercely attacked. A petition and letters of support are published in the review *Der Sturm*. Publication of *A Review of the Past* (Rückblicke) in the *Der Sturm* editions and of *Sounds* (Klänge), 38 poems accompanied by 55 etchings, at Piper's in Munich.
Exhibits for the first time across the Atlantic as part of the Armory Show.

1914
Last exhibition of the Blue Rider, in Berlin. On the declaration of war he leaves Germany and returns to Russia via Zurich, Brindisi, the Balkans and Odessa. Is in Moscow on the 21st of December.
Translation of *The Spiritual in Art* into English.

1915
Moscow and a stay in Sweden. No pictures are painted this year.

1916
Death of Franz Marc at the front. Is separated from Gabriele Münter, meets Nina Andreevsky in a museum. Poems taken from *Sounds* are read in Zurich, during soirées of the Cabaret Voltaire.

1917
Marries Nina Andreevsky on the 11th of February. Trip to Finland.

1918
Member of the fine arts department of the People's Commissariat for Education (Narkompros) directed by Lounatcharsky, teaching in the Moscow Studios for Free Art (Vkhutemas), editor of the journal *Isskoustvo*.
Translation and publication of *A Review of the Past*.
Up until his departure, Kandinsky will be closely involved with the artistic and pedagogic activity arising from the October Revolution. He will paint little during these years.

1919
Members of the committee for the compilation of the Encyclopedia of the Fine Arts. Works on the organizing of museums in Moscow and the provinces. Continues to publish theoretical articles in Germany.

1920
Takes part in the founding of INHUK (Institute of Artistic Culture) where the programme he proposes is voted out which brings with it his resignation. Official exhibition in Moscow. Exhibition in New York.

1921
Continuation and conclusion of his teaching activities in his native country. Seven years to the day after returning there, Kandinsky leaves Moscow and arrives in Germany.

1922
Called to the Weimar Bauhaus in the capacity of professor, he runs the studio for mural painting there, then becomes vice-director.
Sketches for the mural paintings for the state room of the 'Jury-freie' in Berlin. Publication of Kleine Welten (Small Worlds), a collection of twelve prints using varying techniques.

1923
Vice-President of the 'Anonymous Society' of New York. Collaborates in Bauhaus publications.

1924
Founds with Klee, Feininger and Jawlensky the group Die Blauen Vier (The Blue Four).

1925
Transfer of the Bauhaus to Dessau, Kandinsky settles there in June. All these years, up until the second transfer of the Bauhaus, on that occasion to Berlin (in 1932), despite the deterioration of the political atmosphere, are quite calm. His time is divided between teaching and painting itself, with, as always, a large place left for friendship, walks and journeys.

1926
Numerous tributes on the occasion of Kandinsky's sixtieth birthday.
Publication of *Point and Line to Plane* in Munich.

1927
Trips to Switzerland and to Austria. Numerous exhibitions in Germany and abroad, as well as in the following years.

1928
Acquires German nationality. Production for Mussorgsky's 'Pictures from an Exhibition' at the Dessau theatre.

1929
Trip to Belgium, Marcel Duchamp's visit to Dessau, holiday in Hendaye.
First one-man exhibition in Paris, at the gallery Zack.

1930
Exhibits in Paris, at the Galerie de France, and at 'Circle and

Square'.
A stay on the Adriatic, a visit to Ravenna.
1931
Trip to the Middle-East. Mural decoration for the music room at the Berlin International Exhibition.
1932
Transfer of the Bauhaus to Berlin. Trip to Yugoslavia.
1933
In March, closure of the Bauhaus by the Nazis. Kandinsky and Nina decide to go and settle in Paris.
1934
Exhibits at the 'Cahiers d'Art' and at the Jeanne Bûcher gallery. From this year onwards the titles are in French.
1935
Articles in the Cahiers d'Art. Summer on the Côte d'Azur.
1937
Confiscation and putting up for sale by the Nazis of 57 of Kandinsky's works on show in German galleries and considered to be 'degenerate art'.
Visits Paul Klee in Switzerland.
1938
Publishes *Art Concret* in the review *XXᵉ siècle*.
1939
Acquires French nationality.
1940
At the time of the German invasion withdraws for two months to Cauterets, then returns to occupied Paris.
1944
Works up until the month of June. The activity of his last years has been very great: paintings, drawings and watercolours. *Elan tempéré* is his last finished work. He dies on the 13th of December.

PHOTOGRAPH CREDITS

Ch. Bahier, Ph. Migeat, Musée national d'art moderne, Centre Georges Pompidou, Paris: 6, 14, 18, 24, 29, 33, 34, 35, 40, 41, 42, 43. Musée national d'art moderne, Centre Georges Pompidou, Paris: 9, 10, 16, 45, 47, 51, 65, 74, 79, 81, 87, 91, 97, 107, 109, 111, 117, 119, 123, 125, 127, 135, 137. Roger Viollet, Paris: 37. Stedelijk Van Abbe Museum, Eindhoven: 57. Galerie Ernst Beyeler, Bâle: 59. Städtische Galerie im Lanbachhaus, Munich: 63, 69, 71, 75. Museum Boymans-van Beuningen, Rotterdam: 67. Kunstsammlung Nordrhein-Westfalen, Düsseldorf: 99. Galerie Adrien Maeght, Paris: 129. Other photographs are from the collection of Fernand Hazan.

LIST OF ILLUSTRATIONS

67: *Lyrically*, 1911, oil on canvas, 94×130 cm.
Museum Boymans-van Beuningen, Rotterdam.

69: *Romantic Landscape*, 1911, oil on canvas, 94.3×129 cm.
Städtische Galerie im Lanbachhaus, Munich.

71: *Impression IV* (*Gendarme*), 1911, oil on canvas, 95×107.5 cm.
Städtische Galerie im Lanbachhaus, Munich.

73: *Composition IV*, 1911, oil on canvas, 159.5×250.5 cm.
Kunstsammlung Nordrhein-Westfalen, Düsseldorf.

74: *Oars*, 1910, watercolour and Indian ink on vellum, 25×32 cm.
Musée national d'art moderne, Centre Georges Pompidou, Paris.

75: *Improvisation 26* (Rowing), 1912, oil on canvas, 97×107.5 cm.
Städtische Galerie im Lanbachhaus, Munich.

77: *Painting with a Black Arch*, 1912, oil on canvas, 189×198 cm.
Musée national d'art moderne, Centre Georges Pompidou, Paris.

79: *The Last Judgement*, 1912, painting in water and Indian ink under glass, 33.6×45.3 cm.
Musée national d'art moderne, Centre Georges Pompidou, Paris.

81: Study for *Small Pleasures*, 1913, watercolour and Indian ink on laid paper, 23.8×31.5 cm.
Musée national d'art moderne, Centre Georges Pompidou, Paris.

83: *Painting with Red Spot*, 1914, oil on canvas, 130×130 cm.
Musée national d'art moderne, Centre Georges Pompidou, Paris.
Donation Nina Kandinsky.

85: *Painting on Light Ground*, 1916, oil on canvas, 100×78 cm.
Musée national d'art moderne, Centre Georges Pompidou, Paris.
Donation Nina Kandinsky.

87: Untitled (*Achtyrka*), 1917, oil on canvas, 27.5×33.6 cm.
Musée national d'art moderne, Centre Georges Pompidou, Paris.

89: *In Grey*, 1919, oil on canvas, 129×176 cm.
Musée national d'art moderne, Centre Georges Pompidou, Paris.

91: Study for *The Green Border*, 1920, watercolour and Indian ink, 26.9×36.3 cm.
Musée national d'art moderne, Centre Georges Pompidou, Paris.
Donation Nina Kandinsky.

93: *Black Spot*, 1921, oil on canvas, 137×120 cm.
Kunsthaus, Zurich.

95: *Black Grid*, 1922, oil on canvas, 96×106 cm.
Musée national d'art moderne, Centre Georges Pompidou, Paris.

97: Maquette for the Juryfreie Exhibition, 1922, gouache on black paper, 34.7×60 cm.
Musée national d'art moderne, Centre Georges Pompidou, Paris.
Donation Nina Kandinsky.

99: *Through-going Line*, 1923, oil on canvas, 141×202 cm.
Kunstsammlung Nordrhein-Westfalen, Düsseldorf.

101: *In the Black Circle*, 1923, oil on canvas, 130×130 cm.
Collection of Adrien Maeght, Paris.

103: *On White II*, 1923, oil on canvas, 105×98 cm.
Musée national d'art moderne, Centre Georges Pompidou, Paris.
Donation Nina Kandinsky.

105: *Contact*, 1924, oil on canvas, 79×54 cm.
Collection of Adrien Maeght, Paris.

107: *Upward Tension*, 1924, graphite, Indian ink, brown ink and watercolour, 48.7×33.7 cm.
Musée national d'art moderne, Centre Georges Pompidou, Paris.
Donation Nina Kandinsky.

109: *Contrasting Sounds*, 1924, oil on cardboard, 70×49.5 cm.
Musée national d'art moderne, Centre Georges Pompidou, Paris.

111: *Yellow-Red-Blue*, 1925, oil on canvas, 128×201.5 cm.
Musée national d'art moderne, Centre Georges Pompidou, Paris.
Donation Nina Kandinsky.

113: *Accent in Pink*, 1926, oil on canvas, 100.5 × 80.5 cm.
Musée national d'art moderne, Centre Georges Pompidou, Paris.
Donation Nina Kandinsky.
115: *Soft Hard*, 1927, oil on canvas, 33 × 41.5 cm.
Private collection.
117: *On Points*, 1928, oil on canvas, 140 × 140 cm.
Musée national d'art moderne, Centre Georges Pompidou, Paris.
Donation Nina Kandinsky.
119: *Light*, 1930, oil on cardboard, 69 × 48 cm.
Musée national d'art moderne, Centre Georges Pompidou, Paris.
121: *Thirteen Rectangles*, 1930, oil on cardboard, 69.5 × 59.5 cm.
Musée national d'art moderne, Centre Georges Pompidou, Paris.
123: *Two Green Points*, 1935, oil and sand on canvas, 114 × 162 cm.
Musée national d'art moderne, Centre Georges Pompidou, Paris.
Donation Nina Kandinsky.
125: *The White Line*, 1936, gouache, tempera on black paper, 49.9 × 38.7 cm.
Musée national d'art moderne, Centre Georges Pompidou, Paris.
127: *Composition IX*, 1936, oil on canvas, 113.5 × 195 cm.
Musée national d'art moderne, Centre Georges Pompidou, Paris.
129: *Centre with Accompaniment*, 1937, oil on canvas, 114 × 146 cm.
Collection of Adrien Maeght, Paris.
131: *Many-coloured Ensemble*, 1938, oil and enamel paint on canvas, 116 × 89 cm.
Musée national d'art moderne, Centre Georges Pompidou, Paris.
Donation Nina Kandinsky.
133: *Composition X*, 1939, oil on canvas, 130 × 195 cm.
Kunstsammlung Nordrhein-Westfalen, Düsseldorf.
135: *Sky Blue*, 1940, oil on canvas, 100 × 73 cm.

Musée national d'art moderne, Centre Georges Pompidou, Paris.
Donation Nina Kandinsky.
137: *Reciprocal Accord*, 1942, oil and enamel paint on canvas, 114 × 146 cm.
Musée national d'art moderne, Centre Georges Pompidou, Paris.
Donation Nina Kandinsky.
139: *Tempered Elan*, 1944, oil on cardboard, 42 × 58 cm.
Musée national d'art moderne, Centre Georges Pompidou, Paris.